Novel=
IN-THE-MAKING

Also by Mary O'Hara

MY FRIEND FLICKA

THUNDERHEAD

GREEN GRASS OF WYOMING

THE SON OF ADAM WYNGATE

Novel=
IN-THE-MAKING

by Mary O'Hara

DAVID McKAY COMPANY, INC.
NEW YORK

Manufactured in the United States of America

Van Rees Press • New York

Novel-
IN-THE-MAKING

One

ALL MY LIFE I have kept diaries. Not regularly but in-
termittently. Sometimes brief bulletins, sometimes long
analyses. While I am writing a novel, the diary concerns
itself chiefly with the problems of the work. The more
difficult the problems, the more deeply analytical are the
entries in the diary. I write myself out of the jams.

My last book, *The Son of Adam Wyngate,* was the most
difficult book I have ever written. I described a drama
seen through the foreground action of half a dozen dancing figures. It took me three years.

When it had been published and exhaustively reviewed
and I had arrived at a detached and almost disinterested
attitude toward it, I read over the notes and diary entries
I had made during the writing, and realized I had material here for what would actually be a journal of the job.

Did I care to do such a book? Would anyone want to
read it? I seldom finish a page without wondering if there
is anything on it that will make a reader turn to the next.
An author, I feel, ought to be read. It has always astonished me to hear it said that the artist works for himself

only, to express himself. That there is a therapeutic catharsis in this I do not deny. A pleasure too, *ergo* my diaries and my hours of improvisation at the piano. It is possible that one's best work is done in this sort of secret freedom, but I doubt it. And isn't it considered rather peculiar to talk to yourself?

Craftsmanship enters in when out of the free and apparently limitless outpourings is distilled a statement, something carefully punctuated and shaped with beginning, middle, and end. It must contain the essence of that wide creative impulse and must be so artfully composed that the message is communicable. Thus it can become a book; or a sonata; be put on a shelf; endure.

Who would read such a journal if I wrote it? I could only judge by myself. Long before I had written my first novel I had been interested in methods and techniques. Any book with such a title as this would have caught my eye.

A teacher of literature told me it would be valuable for classroom work. Some of the greatest writers, Chekhov and Tolstoi, kept diaries on the progress of their work. And since writing is as individual as personality, the record of how a difficult novel comes off for one writer, what particular obstacles are met and overcome, must be in a sense unique, and therefore a genuine contribution.

It would necessarily be in the form of an autobiography; for, while a book is being written, things happen to the author that affect it. Do we not often wonder what causes a sudden change of pace or mood in a book? A critic said of a short story of mine, "As she neared the end she began to write as if she was running to catch a train." Perhaps I was.

To begin with I shall present a few entries made in my diary before I had even decided to write the Wyngate book but was actually midway of another. This was back in 1948, late August; and I was moving from California to Connecticut, driving the three thousand and some miles on the Lincoln Highway, or U.S. 30.

U.S. 30

. . . making this trip in my gray Ford sedan . . . a removal on a grand scale, for my adult life has been spent in the West as a married woman . . . it is to be ended in the East and single, except for Kim.

Kim was a border or working collie, low-slung, black, flecked with brown and white, short-nosed, broad-browed, ready for business, a one-man dog, not to be trusted by strangers. For his comfort I had spread out on the seat of the tonneau a quite luxurious hooked rug splashed with red roses.

Kim is addicted to rugs. I have only to lay one down anywhere for him to stretch out on it. But on this trip he has abandoned his rug. The small luggage is piled on the floor of the tonneau, and Kim finds he can stand on this at just the right level to bring his hot face close to my ear. The thermometer is a hundred and two. The window at my side is open. And though the wind that pours in could be from the maw of a burning fiery furnace, yet it does pour, and there is the illusion of being fanned. Kim, by means of his wide open mouth and long hanging pink tongue, directs a stream of saliva down the back of my neck with accuracy. For the first

[5]

few hundred miles I struggled with him to make him cease this, go back and recline on his rug . . . now I have given up. . . .

All my household furniture had been packed into a Mayfair van before I left Santa Barbara. That van was traveling eastward somewhere on this same U.S. 30; whether ahead of me or behind I had no idea.

The book on which I was at work had been begun a year earlier in California under the scratch title of *The California Story*, and I had, of course, announced this to my publishers. They had wired congratulations and from time to time had sent pleasant letters, designed to cheer me on. During the year one of the editorial board had come in person to Santa Barbara. He saw some chapters of the new book and carried the word back that it was about yogis.

My publishers don't think much of yogis. (They are wrong in this. Yogis are coming in more and more.) But they did not let me know of their disapproval until long after, and I continued work on the book until I was interrupted by events of a personal nature.

Better not have personal things happen to you when you are writing a book. Don't play an active part in life; be a spectator. But that I could not do. Often the whole of my thought was given over to emergencies and crises. Then, when I would come back to the book, the fictional events and characters had lost substance and no longer moved freely.

But now I was properly detached. I had typewriter and

[6]

briefcase with me in the car. In the briefcase was a big Manila envelope that held all that had been written of *The California Story*. I had intended doing a few hours' work every evening when the day's run was over.

It is difficult to find the right sort of sleeping place for Kim and me. There must be a roadside cabin with some grass and trees at least on one side and on that same side must be a window looking out from the room I am to occupy. . . . There is a little ritual we perform. I take Kim to his comfortable spot in the grass under the tree and tie him there with a long rope; then I go inside, look out the window and speak to him from it . . . he waits for that . . . then he lies down with his eyes on that window and when he hears the typewriter he is content. . . .

But I'm not getting on with *The California Story* . . . so far all I've done is arrange the things on the table, write a little in this diary, then plant my elbows, prop my face in my hands, and sit there motionless until fatigue overcomes me and I stagger to bed. . . .

Publishers are flattering and indulgent toward their authors. Yet they keep pushing them a little. Perhaps it's a good thing. *Green Grass of Wyoming,* my last novel, was published in 1946. They have been telling me these last years that if I don't bring out another soon I will be forgotten.

"They" were two of the editors of the J. B. Lippincott Co., Mark Haverford, the tall, sunburned, yachtsman Quaker; and Frank Niven, the manager, suave, handsome, and careful.

[7]

There was also associated with them at that time, the editor of *Story Magazine,* Whit Burnett—explosive literary genius with a goatee.

This was really my second novel that I was facing, for the first three books had been one long story with the same characters and same locale.

The second novel is the great hazard for any novelist. If a first novel succeeds, publishers, critics, public are expectant. What are you writing now? How soon will it come out? Everyone, including you yourself, takes it for granted that now you have proved you are a novelist you will go on novelizing and make a career out of it. So you cast about for something that will be as good as your first and discard one idea after the other.

U.S. 30

... but a story has to compel you. ... *California Story* is not compelling me at all ... it seems remote from me, written by someone else ... too much has happened to me and I am no longer the same person. ... What book then?

How much heat can a long-haired dog stand? What would be the symptoms of heat prostration? We start in the early morning. By one o'clock I am desperately looking for shade ... a few trees, some deep grass, or a hedge of bushes. ... When I find it, I pull off the road and Kim and I creep into the greenery. ... He won't eat. He disappears, he is motionless. I stretch out ... put my face in the grass. ... We let the sun slide down the western sky. At six I have wasted, oh, so much time and his majesty is ready to eat. I open his can of Pard ... mix it with his meal. He wolfs it, occasionally pausing to look up at me with slowly waving brush. We take to the road again, stopping at the first filling station for Kim to drink. I drive till the light begins to fade (don't like night driving). Lucky there are no speed limits on these long empty midwestern roads, but my car begins to vibrate unpleasantly at sixty-five. At this rate it will take me a fortnight to cross the continent. . . . Yes. . . . What book then?

Two

IN A NOVEL I always set my fictional characters in a real geographical locale, and one with which I am familiar. I have lived on the East Coast, West Coast, and Rocky Mountain Divide; so I had those three locales.

I have written about the Rocky Mountain Divide and done all I can do with the Wyoming weathers and plains and thundering herds.

Nobody seems to believe this. They are even indignant at the idea that I would write about anything else and doubtful that I could.

In London, a couple of years ago, I explained with some heat to the head of the Lippincott branch there that, in my opinion, *My Friend Flicka,* the first of the trilogy, had been the very core of a tightly wound spring, crowded with potentialities. *Thunderhead,* the second book, had explored some of those potentialities, sweeping in wider, thinner circles. *Green Grass of Wyoming* was on the outer periphery, not nearly so contained, so inevitable. Should I then go on for a dozen more sequels, thinning and emasculating my original material? He answered calmly that, yes, I should; for they would still be profitable for everyone; it was inconceivable to abandon such a vein of gold.

Even more pressure was exerted on me by the many hundreds of fan letters I received from all over the world, from English children playing with their ponies in South Africa, from young American pilots on war missions over Italy, from a hospital bed in Malaya, from a library deep in the bowels of a battleship in the Pacific Ocean, all showering me with gratitude and begging me to go on with more tales of the Goose Bar Ranch and Flicka and Ken.

I so loved that world—the high plateau teeming with life, lifted up under the inverted blue bowl of the Wyoming skies—that I might have gone on writing about it had not my hero, Ken, who was ten years old in the first of the three books, managed in some unaccountable way to grow up and get himself engaged in the third. Was I to have as hero a young man accomplished with razors and strops? Speaking in a bass voice? Trying to make the football team at college?

In all the hundreds of letters I received, only one of my correspondents was aware of this problem—I think he was about twelve himself; and he solved it with one fine free gesture. After bidding me continue the series, he adjured me not to let Ken grow up and added, "You are making him old beyond his years."

Lacking such courage, and, perhaps, the magic wand, I had turned my back on the Goose Bar Ranch and the Rocky Mountain Divide.

Now it appeared I was turning my back on California too; and *The California Story*.

Kim simply hates this car. Second or third day out after the first water stop in the morning he refused to return to it. I had him on the leash for a little promenade. Leading him back to that mass of heated metal was like leading him up to a furnace. Ten feet away he sat down and cast me a quizzically reproachful glance. I pulled lightly on the leash and said, "Now Kim come on" . . . and pulled harder. He allowed his head to yield but his weight (and it's considerable) leaned back, anchoring him. "Well, then, let's try the other door." To show he was reasonable he trotted around the back of the car with me but at the strategic moment cast me that look and sat down again. The gas station attendants gathered to see the outcome. In such contests with animals or children I have found one must simply persevere. I don't know how many times Kim and I walked around the car . . . at last he got in. . . .

Now it is a daily game . . .

There came a night when, having found a suitable cabin and engaged a room, I returned to the car for my overnight bag and typewriter. As I reached for the brief-case that held *The California Story,* I hesitated. Was there any use? Was I ever going to finish it or even write another page of it?

I closed the door of the car and stood there thinking. Kim, seated on his haunches on the rose-splashed hooked rug, kept his eyes steadily upon me.

Within five minutes the decision was made, and I never thereafter questioned it again. I was through with *The California Story.*

I had now to think about my next book and plan it.

Certain important decisions must be made before a novel can be begun. The first of these, the *locale,* had made itself by a process of elimination. Not Rocky Mountain Divide—not California; it would be, then, somewhere on the East Coast.

I now asked myself if I should tell the story in the first person, as if it were an autobiography, or in the third person from the point of view of what is technically called the omniscient author.

Wheels turning under me have always made wheels turn in my mind. And the world on each side of U. S. 30 was vast and empty. I found myself able to think clearly and easily.

I had once seen a young woman pick up a new book and glance at the opening, which went as follows: "When I opened my eyes that first morning of my married life—" She immediately closed the book and put it down, exclaiming, "Oh, it's an I-book."

I asked, "You prefer the omniscient-author point of view?"

She didn't understand the term; and I had to explain that it meant the author wrote in the third person, as God; someone outside the story, knowing all about everyone, even their thoughts. For who but God (or the hero himself) would know what he was thinking as he opened his eyes on the first morning of his married life?

Yes, she said, that was what she liked. The other way, written in the first person, pretending to be the actual experience of the author, you would know that it could never be as interesting as a story told by someone outside the book who knew all about everyone in it.

Though I agreed, I argued the other side. In an I-book, there was the close identification of the writer (*ergo* reader) with the hero. Who can be closer to a hero than himself? Well, is that really true? A mother knows more about a boy than he knows himself, and if she were God, more than he ever *could* know. God could know, for instance, as the boy walked down the forest path, that around that corner lay a danger, or an occasion of glory, or the end of everything; could describe the boy's steps, feelings, thoughts, fears, quite as well as the boy himself; and at the same time all that lay ahead around the bend; could glimpse and let the reader glimpse the state of mind of the mother waiting at home, her appearance, thoughts, a bit of her past; could go as far afield as he liked, perhaps showing that a neighbor was also walking through the woods and would intersect the boy's path in a few moments for good or ill. . . . Yes, a far wider scope.

Moreover, faces are interesting; and vivid descriptions of them in books are interesting, too. But there can be no description of the hero's face if he is telling the story himself. For instance, he could hardly say, "My face was beautiful with the young look of wildness and freedom and my dark blue dreaming eyes." But change the first person to the third as omniscient author would write it, and it becomes, "His face was beautiful with the young look of wildness and freedom and his dark blue dreaming eyes." And this was a sentence in the first chapter of *My Friend Flicka,* which the publishers chose to use as a blurb on the book jacket.

The omniscient-author point of view, moreover, can always include the autobiographical. The boy could say, "Dad, I was walking down that path through the woods yesterday, and suddenly I heard . . ." and a whole episode can thus be told in the first person, if the author so wills.

There was still another drawback to an I-book, to my mind the worst of all; namely, that there can be presented only the speech, grammar, dialect of the one single character—the hero (or whoever is chosen to recount the tale). This can create a monotony that is almost unbearable, especially if it *is* dialect. Such books may have good plots, characters, incidents, and atmosphere, but yet be hard to read, though perhaps easier to write. For the author puts blinders on himself and recounts only what happens from a single point of view—his own.

There is that saying, "Hard writing makes easy reading."

I want my books to be easy to read. It seems presumptuous to expect a reader to do heavy labor to get at my meaning.

Three

A THOUSAND MILES or more ran under my wheels during my long examination of the question of the point of view.

From the start, I saw that I leaned toward omniscient author.

The three novels I had already written had all been told in the third person, and I began to wonder if it was merely that I did not want to experiment with something new; or whether, being the kind of writer I am, it was really best for me? I decided finally that this was the case, and for two reasons, both very important to me.

First, it is my opinion that the omniscient-author point of view creates more suspense, since God may be worried about us, seeing disaster approach, while we are still placid and unknowing in the rocking chair. I would never be one to minimize the importance of suspense. I like exciting stories whether I am writing them or reading them.

Second, in an I-book, there can be no narrative except what the narrator narrates, and the narrator is the hero, the I.

All the reflections, soliloquies, philosophical comments, descriptions, deductions, must emerge from the brain and lips of that one character, or someone he hears talking. And heroes of I-books being, as they are, but mere mortal men, and inside the book—one of the cast—cannot talk very freely without going out of character. Only someone outside the book, the omniscient-author-narrator, could say all I wish to say.

I admit this is a good deal, perhaps more than it ought to be, for I do like to air my opinions and reflections and philosophical observations.

When, back in 1940 at my Wyoming ranch, I decided that I must really try to put some of my story ideas into marketable shape, I went to New York and joined a summer extension course at Columbia. The lecturer was Whit Burnett. The course was for two hours in the morning, two in the afternoon, for five days a week, and it lasted for six weeks—my first classroom experience. Most of the students were undergraduates or young teachers.

I had already done professional writing; but it was screen writing and in Hollywood before I moved to Wyoming. Everyone tells you this does not teach you how to write, it teaches you how not to. I do not agree. You can learn character, plot, dramatic construction, editing, visualization.

But there is one thing you cannot do in screen writing or radio or stage or any form of dramatic writing: you cannot indulge in author-narrative, because there isn't any. And this, as I have said, I longed to do. The only form of writing that would permit me this indulgence was short stories or novels. I did not aspire to novels. I thought only gods and goddesses wrote novels. But I did think I could learn to write publishable short stories, so joined this class.

Mr. Burnett's method was to ask for unsigned stories, read them aloud without disclosing the author, then invite discussion.

I was indignant when, after reading a story of mine, he asked what was the matter with it, and with one voice the class answered, "Too much author."

What had I come to New York for? Just to go on with dramatic writing? I'd never go to school for *that!* I'd been doing it for years!

So I argued the point, and there was a lively discussion. Mr. Burnett said, "I wouldn't want you all to write like radio writers, but—" But really he did. *The scene.* Write the scene. How many thousands I had done for the movies!

I had brought with me to New York several finished short stories. One of them was *My Friend Flicka* in about five thousand words. During that summer class at Columbia I turned this story in, and it made a sensation. I must admit it was written in sharply dramatized form—practically no author-narrative.

Mr. Burnett was not only the professor of this class and editor of *Story Magazine;* he had established his own publishing imprint called the Story Press; and whenever he "discovered" some promising newcomer, he would act as liaison between such an author and a publishing house. He now wanted to publish *My Friend Flicka* in his magazine; also wanted me to make a novel of it for Lippincott, or write a new one out of similar Wyoming material.

[18]

"But I could never write a novel," I objected.

"You can write stories."

"That's different."

"No. You just keep on. As if every story is one chapter."

"I'm sure I couldn't."

"Of course you could. And if you get stuck, we'll all gather around and help you."

We were, during this conversation, at lunch together, Mark Haverford, Frank Niven, Whit Burnett, and I. I would not promise. They offered inducements, a contract with an advance, but it seemed impossible to me.

In the end, everything happened as Whit had hoped, though I did not sign the contract until the book was finished. Not till then could I really believe I would achieve it.

This bit of past history is linked to the subject of author-narrative. For when I began to write the novel *My Friend Flicka,* I remembered the lesson I had learned in Whit's summer class, and told myself, Do it in scenes. Mind, now! No author-narrative—and I got into endless difficulties. I would get *into* scenes and could never get *out*—and I complained to Whit, and he answered blithely, "Why, just do all that in author-narrative—as you have it in your notes."

So then I understood. You do but you don't. And this paradox cheered me. Almost everything important in life *is* and at the same time *isn't*.

This challenges your skill.

Done to excess, I saw, author-narrative is old-fashioned and boring. But properly controlled, it is practical machinery; and, put mostly through the thoughts and words of the characters, with only a modicum straight from the author, provides just that weight and depth without which a novel is only skin deep.

Four

Two of the important decisions had now been made. The *locale;* the *point of view.*

Next I had to decide what my new book would be about. That is what they ask you, "What's it about? What is the subject?"

The Flicka books had been about horses.

Anyone might choose such a subject as horses to write about just because horses are beautiful; because they are universally beloved. But aside from liking them you have to know a great deal about them. You have to have what I called a "body of thought" about them.

This body of thought is likely to be the result of years of study or close observation. Worthwhile thoughts do not originate in a typewriter or pour off the point of a pen, or spring into being just because someone has majored in English and has the ambition to be a writer. They are accumulated during years of living, thinking, reflecting, and, often, taking notes.

Unless an author happens to have had vastly wide and differentiated experiences, or is a walking encyclopedia of knowledge, there are not going to be many fields in which he has a body of thought ready and waiting. So we find young mothers writing about children; psychiatrists about mental cases; lawyers, stories with a legal slant, etc.

I had had a sufficient body of thought about horses to write about them successfully. Did I have it about anything else? Yes, I thought I did. About religion. And about music.

U.S. 30

... tonight I'm going to write something which may turn out to be very important. ... I've been thinking about that body of thought which is going to fill my next book, and have decided it had better be the religion. If I'm not ready for it now I never will be. I have hundreds of pages of notes filed away ... have been wondering all day why I wrote those notes? Why was I sufficiently interested? Why am I like this? Why did I spend years studying the Sacred Books of the East and going to lectures on mysticism? What gives the answer, of course, is my whole life ... it is a thread that has run all through it ... the inner need which compelled me ... *there* was compulsion!

I must write all this out. ...

If I decide to write about religion ... and I think I am deciding ...

I have almost decided ... then it must be very clear to me why I am doing it and exactly what the foundation of the book will be ... how the religious thought of my life will be related to the religious thought in the book. ... This will amount to a brief spiritual autobiography ... here it is. ...

How far back should this reminiscence go? I would like to reach the seed that eventually flowers in the book I am about to write. I see that it goes beyond the span of my own life.

The young son of a Philadelphia Quaker family, Reese Fell Alsop, was attending a Quaker college when he received an inner call that caused him to abandon his church and the legal career he was planning and enter the Episcopalian ministry. This was my father.

My earliest recollections are of the big house in Brooklyn Heights and the church of which my father was the rector, St. Ann's. We were a large family of several generations, for my mother died when I was six and my grandmother, Mrs. James Walton Spring (Mary O'Hara Spring), and some aunts came to live with us.

For generations back apparently, our family—Alsops, Springs (Gardiner Spring of the Brick Church, New York), Dennys (Father Denny, Jesuit priest), Edwards (Jonathan and Timothy), Penns (William), and Fells—have been adventurers of the spirit, always searching their souls, never hesitating to declare the truth as they see it, even at the cost of becoming exiles and wanderers.

In my own case the soul searching began in childhood. I was taught religion not only at Sunday school, in church, at prayer meetings, at chapel in school, and at daily morning prayers in our own house, but by every member of the household including servants, each with a different version, different, that is, in the degree of unpleasant prohibition imposed on a small child, but quite the same, it seemed to me, in that it was a way of thinking and living that was bound to take most of the fun out of life.

I wondered if such strict piety, and so much of it, went more than skin deep. Looking around, I saw that many of those who taught me lost tempers, prevaricated when it suited their purpose, were worldly, proud, and selfish.

But if this religion did not command my faith and obedience, what then did I believe in? Now began the soul searching.

One day when I was fourteen or fifteen, I closed my lips when, at morning prayers, the Creed was recited. It never occurred to me that the silence of one voice among so many would be noticed, but to my horror my father stopped the ceremony to look at me and say, "You're not saying the Creed, Mary."

I stubbornly remained silent, and he stubbornly waited. Every eye was on me. At last I said, "But I don't believe all that."

From that day on I felt I was outside. Not that I minded. Far from being afraid or troubled, I was restive as a young colt to get out and away—to find a new life, new ways, a new and wider air.

Hoping to convert me, my father placed in my room a great pile of heavy tomes, which he explained were Scotch theological works. But one glance at the fine print and solid pages of unbroken paragraphs was enough for me, and I politely returned them to his study. He then decided to take the matter lightly and nicknamed me Prodigal Daughter.

I well knew the parable of the Prodigal Son who wasted his substance in foreign lands and became a swineherd, but I fell in line with my father's joke and laughed when he would greet me at breakfast with, "How's the Prod this morning?"

When I was nineteen, I became engaged to a young

man who was also an unbeliever. My father did not approve. But as I had, the year before, inherited a small income from my grandmother's estate, I was independent. We were married and went to California to live.

The Prodigal had now arrived in those foreign lands. The story proceeded. Most of my substance was, one way or another, wasted, and the marriage did not endure. There I was, at last, alone and stranded, with two little ones to care for.

To tide me over until I should somehow get on my feet, I was allowed to draw advances from the family estate.

There is a familiar story, that of the person who strives —succeeds fabulously, only to find emptiness and hunger at the core of his new life. The strangeness of my experience was that having failed, I somehow saw that even had I succeeded—even if I had the world in my hand—there would have been this same emptiness. There simply were no human solutions to human problems. I needed something other than the human and the material, and what else was there? Nothing. I sank into complete despair.

I pushed the baby's pram, looking up at the sky line, the craggy peaks that hang over Los Angeles, and words remembered from the many Sundays sitting in the pew at St. Ann's moved through my mind. "I will lift up mine eyes unto the hills, from whence cometh my help." My suffering was extreme, and it went on for many years.

But the soul searching, begun in childhood, continued, and ever more deeply. I occasionally read my Bible and paused at St. Paul's words, "I die daily."

When all human, natural, and intellectual sustenance

is taken away, you find other bread to eat, or you starve. I found that, whether or not I was agnostic, I did believe in an eventual, all-conquering Good. But churches, I still thought, were unnecessary, and provided the letter but not the spirit.

There around me in California current thought was bubbling with those ideas that have now, after many decades, fought their way into orthodoxy in the eastern states under the name of psychosomatic medical practice.

Teachings from cults named Unity, New Thought, Mental Science, as well as Christian Science and Theosophy, poured from some inexhaustible source and gathered converts by the thousands. All of these teachings derived from India and Tibet and had been brought to this country by the missionary efforts of Hindu swamis and yogis.

Centers and schools of these Eastern philosophies were numerous, and their systems of physical exercises were studied and practiced. To meet a turbaned Hindu on the street or sitting cross-legged in the forest, in meditation, would cause no surprise; nor a large sign by the roadside with an arrow pointing into the woods and the single word *ASHRAM* (retreat).

This had been going on in California since the turn of the century and before. I now found reference to it everywhere. Lafcadio Hearn, lecturing at the University of Tokyo in 1890 (these lectures later were published), said of Sir Thomas Browne, "In his writings there are suggestions and thoughts that seem much too large for orthodox Christianity, but which would excellently illustrate the teachings of the older, eastern religions." To find such authority as this for my own growing convictions was exciting. And I was finding it everywhere.

That modern psychological thought has had the trail blazed by yoga philosophy is now stated by writers too numerous to mention. (One book, for instance, *The Meeting of East and West* by F. S. C. Northrop of Yale, New York Macmillan Co., 1946.) But it was all new to me then. And if this was religion, it was a most interesting kind. I loved the physical exercises designed to perfect balance, co-ordination, posture, keep the body pliable and strong, and prolong youth. On the wide California beaches, sunburned American boys and girls practiced the deep breathing, the strange attitudes. I loved the mental exercises to achieve control of the mind—for, obviously, right thinking comes before right doing; and right feeling before thinking; and willing before feeling. Heretofore religion had told me what to do, even against my will. Now I had to see what I must think—feel—will. And learn and practice new techniques that would enable me to do it.

This—the *interior* religious life—I might just as easily have discovered in a Christian convent. But it happened to me as I have said.

The most important steps in life are often those taken most carelessly. I went one day with a friend to hear a certain lecturer, and my whole life was changed. He was an Irishman of fifty or sixty; but he looked exactly like a brown-faced Hindu with the nose of Savonarola and burning dark eyes.

He became a second father to me, my spiritual director. (He is dead now.)

[27]

no church, no guru, no lectures. A universal church, I now saw, accessible to all, was a necessity.

Since my study of the early Christian fathers I had held the opinion that the Roman Catholic Church had preserved more of the doctrines and practices of antiquity than the Protestant. I had sent my daughter to a Catholic convent for her education, and we often discussed the possibility of her entering that church. When she went away from home to college, her decision, of which I approved, was taken. Some years later the Ecclesiastical Court of the Church annulled my first marriage, and I followed her in.

During all these changes, I had never ceased my religious studies, readings, and note takings. I knew that sooner or later I would write about this.

The writing of the three Wyoming books did not interrupt that determination. Those simple stories, translated into many languages, including Braille for the blind and a version to be pictured on the ceilings of hospitals for the bedfast, have evoked a response from all over the world that is puzzling. My own explanation is, they were drenched with that other-worldly air, the air that children and innocents breathe, the air that I myself had been seeking for twenty years.

U.S. 30

It's a bright moonlight night . . . just went to the window and looked out at Kim. A dark splotch in the shadow of a tree. There's the gleam of an eye. I spoke to him . . . saw the slight movement from the shadow where his tail is and caught that sound he makes—a high-pitched, strained, nearly inaudi-

[30]

ble sound, as if he is obliged to burst through a dimension to speak to me. . . .

It's late tonight . . .

I've made a beginning at last . . . yes, I've decided. . . .

Five

EVERYBODY, they say, has one good novel in them—their own autobiography.

I had promised Lippincott that someday I would write them a novel about Brooklyn in the early decades of this century. They wanted this because, when I had written a bit of autobiography for publicity purposes, they took a liking to the scenes of myself as a little girl walking the Brooklyn Bridge with my clergyman father, sitting at the crowded dining-room table listening to my elders talk.

But what would I put into a Brooklyn novel? Period writing has never interested me; I cannot see drama in changing styles in clothes and manners; I like the un-changing and universal movements of the human soul.

Besides, I had no intention of writing an autobiography in novel form.

So far, I have never done this. Nor is any book of mine the life story of anyone I ever knew or heard of. Not, that is, the story or plot.

But every sentence that comes from an author's mind, written or spoken, is drawn from a reservoir within him that has been stocked by his observations, memories, imaginings, readings, deductions.

Dramatic incidents are all around us, drawn into that reservoir by our five senses. This is the raw material of books. But in fragments.

When we wish to write a complete story, we draw out these fragments, put them together artfully, supply missing parts by invention, and give the whole unity and meaning by putting our personal stamp on it.

The author's taste will choose the subject; his philosophy provide the message; his experience the body of thought. And a few of the subsidiary characters can be taken from life; namely, those who do not move the plot, who are present merely for color, or humor, or incident.

As, in *My Friend Flicka,* the little wrangler. And the doctor. That doctor was a friend of mine in real life. He took out my appendix. He told me that the day my book went on sale in Cheyenne, his phone rang all morning. "Did you know that Mary has put you in her book?"

The reason I could not write autobiography is because my novels are fables and have a message.

This is not very popular today. A good deal of advice is addressed to novelists telling them an artist should not deliver messages, should just entertain; depict life; make no point, point no moral; get nowhere special because life gets nowhere special.

I do try not to be too obvious with my message, but I've had children to bring up; I have opinions and principles; and I couldn't write a book that did not make a definite point. The happenings in the story must illustrate that point; the characters must be those to whom, logically, such things would happen. I go on the theory that there is a close connection between people and the things that happen to them. So of course I have to invent my principal characters.

There seems to be in the world today great hesitation or unwillingness to make or subscribe to any sort of statement or message; so that speech, ideas, performances, music, philosophies, hang unfinished, without logical end. Such a novel may have interesting characters, places, episodes, situations—all lifelike and depicted with skill. Possibly it's good reading, at least a certain amount of it. But I am disappointed if, in the end, it does not say anything. And how does he know when he is done? How does he know when *he has said it?*

Well, each to his own way. I would have to know the full meaning of my tale and the point of it; and the moment *when I had said it.*

... the book about religion then. That is to be it. But what about it? What aspect of it? You could not even begin a novel about religion without knowing the central theme. Witch-hunting? The inquisition? A woman who takes Communion in a five-thousand-dollar mink coat? Or the pros and cons of a celibate clergy? .... No. I shall write about mysticism ... that aspect of religion which has always interested me most ... define it now. ...

An intensification of the interior life of meditation and prayer to the point where another sense is developed, a spiritual intuition, disclosing a transcendental aspect of the world and human existence.

When I had written *Flicka*, a critic wrote, "This is a great love story."

In *Green Grass of Wyoming* I wished to define what I meant by the love of God, and put a little dissertation into the letter of the mother to the son going away to school.

That letter caught the attention of publishers, critics, the reading public. Among my fan letters was one from a woman that said that she had made occasion to read that letter to her brother who was a priest. He exclaimed, "I have always known it! Often read of it! But never—" and tears overflowed his eyes.

Love is the theme of all my books because it is the theme of my own life and of human life as I see it. I abhor sentimentality, but I never cease to marvel at the miracles love can perform. It can heal disease; take the insane out of asylums; subdue wild beasts of actual physical jungles as well as of the heart—hatred, envy, pride, malice—and flood the world with happiness.

And I mean love of all kinds. My book should have divine love, and passionate love between men and women, and love of parents for children; and whatever terrible predicament the story would get my hero into, *love* should bring him out.

U.S. 30

Imagine an author talking to the editorial board of a New York publishing firm and, when asked, What is the theme of your novel? answering, Love saves. . . . How polite they would be . . . how solemn. Imagine the huddle after they had left the author. One of them might say, "But it might be box-office . . . it's just corny enough." If they accepted it on that basis, they would want it to be corny. In fact, there are many who would not recognize as religion anything that was not corny. But my book will not be corny.

I think it is getting hotter. Kim's tongue continues to hang out . . . we are approaching the eastern states and there is more traffic . . . I detour the big towns.

I began to think about my characters. There is bound to be a good deal of theology in such a book, and this seems a more masculine subject than feminine. My hero, I thought, would be a clergyman; or a man thinking of taking orders; or one expelled for some reason from the Church.

There occurred to me small scenes, little real-life vignettes when priests have talked to me simply and frankly and confidentially over a cup of after-dinner coffee, or a visit in the garden. One, in his late middle years, confided that temptation had never been mitigated for him—the temptation to drink immoderately. Another, that for him, the violence of the sex drive during his early manhood had nearly cost him his reason. Another, his despair when he found he had, truly, no vocation. Another . . . "I have always thought there could be nothing so wonderful in the world as to have a nice wife."

But these were Catholic priests. I had not been a Catholic long enough to be familiarly acquainted with every detail of a priest's life as cradle Catholics are. A Protestant clergyman then. I had known many besides my own father. I remembered one who preached in the village church one summer of long ago—a young fellow. I couldn't take in a thing he said, I was so affected by the despair on his face. What was the matter? Had he lost his faith? Or committed the unforgivable crime? Did he covet his neighbor's wife?

The miles running westward under my wheels did not banish that face, the gaunt, dark young face, crucified with its inner torture. It was long ago, and I never knew his name, nor have I thought of him from that day to this, but I now felt love for the memory of him. If he were to be my hero, with what tenderness I could explore his trouble and what joy bring him out. A story about him began to build—a shadowy sort of outline. And I made a mental note, *When the hero and theme meet and fuse, the plot begins.*

No . . . he was too young. The things that would happen to him would not be the right things. My hero must be older. The face drifted away into limbo, again forgotten.

U.S. 30

Today I made a sort of highway friend, a pickup of course. A truck with trailer nearly as long as a freight car. We passed each other so often in the emptiness of the long roads, I overtaking him on the slight upgrades, he roaring down upon me at incredible speeds when it was level or downgrade, that at last we began to put up a hand to each other as we went by. As if we said, "We be of one blood, ye and I!"

So Kipling used the theme of love too—as who does not?

Six

THE INTERMINABLE journey was nearing its end.

A great deal of important preliminary work had been done on the book, even though I had not yet either plot or characters.

I think most writers go, consciously, through these same preliminaries.

I don't know why it should be so difficult and so painful. Is it because one feels it should all be done with one gay leap of the mind—and then the actual writing be begun? Or is it because every decision is riddled with doubt?

What I had decided on was as follows:

Locale—East Coast.
Point of view—Omniscient author.
Body of thought—My religious studies.
Subject—Mysticism.
Theme—Power of love.
Protagonist—Protestant clergyman; mystic.

I kept seeing faces as one sees them sometimes—single ones, or groups, or hordes and crowds and parades of them, in that peculiar interval between waking and sleeping. I wondered if any of these faces would be in my book.

When I reached the crowded eastern states, I left U.S. 30 and reduced speed, for there were speed-limit signs now, and occasionally motorcycle police.

... wondering about faces.... Is it really necessary to paint them vividly and in detail in a novel? Writers differ about this ... some do and some don't ... must confess that when an author does not, I, the reader, do it for him ... must absolutely have a definite picture ... then find it upsetting to read on page fifteen that she is black-haired when I've been picturing a blonde ... should I then have allowed her to go faceless all those pages?

A little ten-year-old girl once told me she had received a good mark for a composition she had turned in at school. I asked her how long it was and what she had put into it. She said it was one paragraph, and she put into it the name of a girl and the color of her eyes and hair, where she lived and how old she was. Her voice was satisfied, not to say complacent, as if there was really nothing more to tell.

This is the unsophisticated taste, but is it not sophisticated as well? In fact, universal? Do we not all want to know exactly those things about someone in whom we are interested?

There was an article in the *Saturday Review of Literature* by Charles Morgan that challenged this. He does not like to give the physical descriptions of the faces in his stories. Who does? It is extremely difficult. His argument was that, since the physical face is so soon lost sight of by the other characters in the story, it should be lost sight of by the reader too.

I admit that one can be completely oblivious of physical characteristics. Listening to good conversation, one wouldn't know if the face it came from had blue eyes or black even though one was looking right into it. And yet it seems to me Mr. Morgan's argument is specious. I think he would hate it if his own dear ones lost their physical faces.

The heat did not abate. I began to see water shimmering at the end of the journey as desert travelers see mirages.

But it was no mirage; it was a memory of my sister Elma's swimming pool where it hides away in the pine grove adjacent to her country place at Tyringham.

As well as a memory it was an anticipation; for Kim and I were headed for that place and that pool; then, after a short cooling-off visit, on to Monroe, Connecticut, where, on an earlier visit, I had bought half of a farm about three miles from Monroe Center. It had an old barn on it, which was first to be moved a hundred yards to a better site, then to be rebuilt into a dwelling. During the coming year I planned to supervise this building and write my book.

I had always wanted to live on or near a New England "green." Monroe Center was such a green, elm-shaded. There was a small white-spired church at each end, and two rectories, one of them an exquisite old house of pale pink brick. The fire house, Masonic Lodge, and town hall filled one side; old colonial dwellings the other.

Among these was the big white salt-box with black shutters belonging to the Russell Masons, and I had leased the upper floor—a roomy, airy apartment—for a year. But before I installed in that apartment the two pieces of furniture from which I did not allow myself to be separated for long—the big steel file that held my papers and manuscripts, and my Mason & Hamlin concert grand piano—I was to cross the Atlantic to visit my son Kent in Paris. He was stationed there and had an apartment in the rue Singer. I would spend two weeks with him, and then we would go together to London, where, on October 21, at St. Martins-in-the-Fields, he was to marry his English Deirdre.

Life was crowding me again.

My Ford sedan was at last climbing the hills of the Berkshires.

We arrived at the swimming pool, the luscious green lawns and hedges, and the loving welcome.

After the visit at Tyringham, Kim and I drove on down to Connecticut and took possession of our new apartment.

The Mayfair van arrived, disgorged the file and the piano, and then went off with the rest of my furniture to put it in storage until my new house should be ready to receive it.

I spent some busy days with the architect who was to do the remodeling job on my barn.

I now had to put Kim in kennels for the term of my absence. In connection with this, there was an episode that lingers in my memory.

The kennels were ideal, set in a roomy clearing in the

forest, and each dog had a room and an open, caged runway for himself. But the building, though practical, was constructed in a rather forbidding manner, the rows of rooms opening off a long central passage, dark and narrow, interrupted at intervals by heavy wire doors.

Most of the rooms were already occupied, and as Kim (on a leash) and I followed the trainer down that dark corridor, the occupants—it seemed a hundred dogs—gave tongue in a mighty welcome to Kim. Shall we call it welcome? It filled me with dismay. . . . But I am not a dog, I thought, perhaps Kim . . .

The trainer walked briskly; she had a large key in her hand. She unlocked a steel door and held it open; we passed through. It clanged shut behind us. Then another. The dogs bayed, yodeled, howled.

Kim suddenly sat down on his haunches and cast me that look.

The trainer stood by, expecting trouble.

I dropped on one knee beside him, grieving for him. I smoothed the top of his satiny head. He looked into my eyes, questioning, and I looked back, telling him, Yes, it had to be . . . but I would come back . . . he must just wait quietly.

He accepted this without further protest, and when I rose to my feet, followed me again calmly. The little interchange had taken about a half minute.

But the trainer, whose business was the training and ordering of dogs, was intrigued. "What did you say to him? What sign did you give him? What word?"

But I had no special sign or word. I just explained to him.

Before I drove away in my car, I went to the outside of his runway to say good-by. The hundred dogs yammered salute. Kim was lying against the side of the cage, his head slightly raised, his eyes looking off and beyond with the ineffable expression of one—whether human being or caged animal—who is set to ignore and endure all that is close and immediate, and simply wait.

He did not move or even turn his head when I drove away.

I sailed on the *Queen Elizabeth* for Cherbourg.

Paris was so cold I spent most of my time in bed with the downy on top of me. But sometimes, with the cold, came brilliant sun, and it was warmer outside than in. Through the wide open windows the vocalizing of Paris poured in. Most insistently of all and long to be remembered were the tootlings of horns and cries of market vendors; and in and through all this such a delicious sound that it brought a smile to hear it—the furious warblings of canaries.

Seven

I SPENT hours talking with Kent about the book. He asked me so many questions perhaps I am writing this journal to answer them.

I explained how, though I still had nothing concrete, I did have a solid foundation, and enumerated my decisions as to locale, body of thought, subject, theme, point of view, and protagonist.

I told him of the length of time it had taken me to make these decisions as the wheels spun under me on my journey across the continent.

"But, Mother, all this sounds just like planning and plugging. What about inspiration? Don't you get a real inspiration for a novel?"

"God forbid that I should get the inspiration before I'm ready for it. They come, sometimes, those sudden conflagrations—bursts of spontaneous combustion—and sweep you away—"

"Do you go along, then?"

"Oh, yes. You dare not refuse a gift. And who knows? You *may* write something wonderful. You have to keep all the windows open, especially at the first. Something good might fly in. Don't refuse anything, because who knows? Who knows?"

"Keep fluid, then."

"Yes."

"But finally you have to get set."

"You do."

"And when do you do that?"

"When I really see what I've got. See it's there."

"How soon do you know that?"

"It usually takes considerable time. From the start I know what the problem is; and I must know the solution too. I often write first the scene or scenes that solve the problem, which of course will come near the end. Just to be sure, before I begin, that it *will* be solved."

"And if you can't solve it you abandon the book?"

"Yes. I would not want to write a book posing a problem that was insoluble. I would like my story to make *some* sense. That does not necessarily mean a happy ending, you know; for sometimes the ending that makes sense is a tragedy.

"I remember a movie they were making at the studio when I was there. An expedition had gone into the arctic regions. Young man and woman in it of course. There came the usual difficulties; food exhausted; dogs run away; guide hurt; then a terrible blizzard. It got very exciting. The dangers were well done. But I began to wonder how on earth they were ever going to get the boy and girl out of this in a credible way."

"How did they?"

"They didn't. They really couldn't. As a matter of fact, it's not difficult to get characters into terrible trouble. What is difficult is to get them out again. You can imagine that if there *had* been some way—credible and original and interesting—it would have made an awfully good and exciting adventure sequence. But the writer and director failed in their inventiveness, and so they decided on a tragic ending as being more artistic."

"And how did the picture end?"

"The boy went out into the storm to hunt for something—help of some kind. He didn't come back. The blizzard got worse. The girl at last went out to find him. Then the boy got back to the tent and found the girl gone. *He* went out to find *her*. Then you would see the alternate shots of the girl staggering through the storm shrieking *his* name, and the boy doing the same shrieking *her* name. That went on for a long time. Then, fade out."

"That was the end?"

"Yes."

"It doesn't seem like an end at all."

"That's it. The picture didn't say anything except that they got lost in the snow, for no purpose of their own or the author's that I could see. I would say that was an example where a situation was created that could not be solved."

"And when you're considering a novel, if you see that you are heading into something like that you just don't write it?"

"Yes. Or if it doesn't seem worth while. That stops me with more stories than anything else. Or if I really don't like it much when I get to know it better. Perhaps I don't like the characters that would have to come into being. Or if I feel I haven't a sufficient body of thought to handle it properly. That often happens. There are books I'd love to write and *could* write if only I knew more. Sometimes I'm tempted just because of the dramatic possibilities, and I begin to write scenes. But I know enough not to go on. I don't want to get serious about a book unless I am pretty sure—pretty sure. . . ."

"You choose your location," Kent said, "and know about how much space you'll need, and clear the land and lay your kindling—plenty of kindling—and then the big logs for the big bonfire, and then stand back and wait for the spontaneous combustion?"

"It's more as if you keep on plugging. Take two sticks and rub them and rub them and keep on rubbing and hoping."

"But you have to keep looking over your shoulder too? In case that conflagration might spring up over there behind you?"

"Yes. All around."

"And, one place or another, you finally get your bonfire."

"You mean inspiration. The spark. But what is it? I once tried to define this to myself. Why do certain people get inspirations and others not? Are those perhaps what are called artists? The artist inspires himself. He can become so heated with desire and love and emotion that the fire comes."

The wedding over, I embarked again on the *Queen Elizabeth* and returned to New York. I stayed there until after Christmas and then went up to Monroe.

The green was snow-covered, spider-crossed with the black boughs and trunks of the old elms.

I got Kim out of kennels. I arranged a writing table for my typewriter; bought boxes of paper and carbon; sharpened pencils. I reread many times all those diary entries and notes I had written on U.S. 30. It amounted almost to an abstract of the book. And it was good. I approved of it. But one more thing was needed before I could begin. Just where on the East Coast would my story be laid?

It must be some place I knew from personal experience. It could be Brooklyn in winter. Or Digby, Nova Scotia, where we had spent many summers. Or North East Harbor where the family had a summer house. Or Deercreek, my grandmother's Pennsylvania estate. Or Cape Cod, or New York, or Long Island. . . .

Morning after morning I got up early, facing the same question and the same indifference about answering it. At five or six o'clock I made my cup of strong coffee, took it into the sitting room, drew the old Boston rocker to the window, and sat there, rocking a bit. Kim lay on the floor at a little distance, his head flattened on his paws, his eyes up and steadily regarding me.

I stared out at the snow-covered green; the elms; the little spired churches. I was not really trying to answer that question, not really working. Writing a book didn't seem important. I couldn't care.

All I needed was to fall in love.

Eight

I HAD OFTEN fallen in love. In fact most of my life has been spent deeply in love with someone or something or both or many things.

But I was not in love now. Every breath seemed a sigh drawn with pain from the deepest level within me.

I had said to Kent, "The artist can inspire himself. He can become so heated with love and desire and emotion that the fire comes."

But no fire came.

I thought of that rushing mighty wind when the fire comes. Thinking of it, I remembered that once, after such a wind had suddenly and all unexpectedly seized me, I had tried to put the experience into verse. I had that verse somewhere—perhaps it might help. . . .

I found the verse and read it.

> Soft feather tip so near my cheek
> Coming so secretly, surprising me,
> Dwelling not—swift to be gone,
> Leaving me love-blinded

Seeking the wing that held the dart
And the wild bird that beat the wild wing
Spreading flame
As in rushing flight it passed
And the far space was empty
Save of pulsing light,
A fiery ichor brimming o'er
To burn and quicken
With a sweetness as of wounds
And slowly ebb.
But wonder stayed. There had it been,
The feather tip that brushed my cheek.

But I couldn't believe it.

The weariness and indifference and sighing lasted a long time. Then came a confluence of small happenings and circumstances that, together, produced the spark and put me to work.

I have a folder in my file labeled Publicity Material. My publishers, and publishers of anthologies that have reprinted my stories, publishers of foreign translations, libraries, schools, frequently ask me for biographical material, which I obediently write for them. So through the years this folder has got very full. Now, when a new request comes, I have only to put in my thumb.

A new request reached me at this time. A reverend father, Catholic, had the job of assembling biographies of Catholic authors for a book soon to be published. He requested mine. I went to my file, and what a plum I pulled out this time!

I stood beside the tall steel box, reading this bit of autobiography in a sort of amazement. I had written it a decade ago and forgotten it. Here were living vignettes, full of charm, the same bits of remembered life-in-childhood that had caused Lippincott to say, Someday you must give us a novel about Brooklyn.

Here were the walks across the Brooklyn Bridge, little girl and clergyman father; the ships moving slowly and massively on either side; here was the big family, crowded dining-room table, the German governess, the stern upbringing.

Just a few pages, but alive. Full of charm.

Was it really? Was I right? Or was this an author's favoritism for the youth of her own rememberings? I must get an outsider's opinion—I flew downstairs; yes, flew. No more lethargy. No more sighs.

Russ has snow-white hair, and his thin face is crinkled all over. He is a mere wisp, five feet six tall, and a hundred and eighteen pounds. But he goes through the house so fast you hardly see him.

Russ Mason was sitting on the sofa in the living room.

A young girl of the neighborhood said of him wonderingly, "Russ Mason old? I never think of him as an old man."

When I had first come to Monroe, I had met Russ's wife, Peggy, before I met him; I heard her downstairs arguing with him, telling him he must come up to my apartment with her and meet me. "It's Mary O'Hara, Russ—who wrote the Flicka books. You simply *must*, Russ."

And I heard his answer in an outraged tone of voice. (It has always made me chuckle.) *"In these pants, Peg!"*

[51]

When he finally came up he was in immaculate stiff starched white ducks.

We became great friends. He confided in me: "Mary, I'm going to be seventy years old—yes, seventy. And I didn't even know I was growing old! Why, do you know, when I had to give my description to the fellow who was making out my identification card, I said, brown hair. And he looked at me and said, 'Brown hair? What's the matter with you? You've got white hair. Snow-white hair.' And I went to the mirror and looked and, say, Mary, the guy was right!"

This was the man sitting on the sofa down there, and I plumped myself beside him and said, "Listen to this, Russ." And I read it to him.

When I had finished, I looked at his face. He exclaimed, like a child, "I wish it was me!" And I remembered that I too, as a child, had given that artless and nostalgic cry; that all children did so when they suddenly found themselves standing at the gate of a world they could not enter.

That was enough for me. If I could create that longed-for world—if I could make others say *I wish it was me*—write such a book that others would be caught into it, as Russ had been—that would be all I could ask.

So now it was not merely East Coast, it was Brooklyn Heights. And Brooklyn Heights in the early years of this century.

As I walked slowly up the narrow carpeted stairs to my apartment, the problem of the principal character, the protagonist, resolved itself. Not my own father, of course, nor any of my clergymen forefathers (they would turn in their graves), nor any other of the many clergymen I had known. This clergyman would have gathered his philosophy from both East and West, ancient and modern, as I had. He must embrace all that seemed to me worth while in all I had learned. And I instantly saw it was too much to be expressed through one character. I would make him father and son. And even two did not seem ample enough, so I added a third, the close friend of the son, the Catholic priest. And now it seemed to me I had the vehicle—a three-person hero for that body of (religious) thought which I wished to pour into the book.

The other thing that had given charm to the pages I had read to Russ was, surely, the big family. I myself was one of four children, and members of two other generations lived with us. I would have even more children, for I loved to write about them. I would have six. The six child characters began the process of coming to life. I saw fleeting glimpses of charming child faces. They moved about as to age and height. I thought of various names— kept changing them. Boys changed into girls and girls into boys.

There has been considerable discussion as to whether or not the book, with its very serious adult problems, was bettered or worsened by being cluttered up with a lot of children. I was aware of this danger from the beginning. Nevertheless I kept the children, not only because I believe a big family is interesting to most people, but because the children would provide a relief from the adult story, which I truly feared would bog down in trite, over-emotional melodrama if I did not find a way to overlay it with casual, lifelike movement.

For in reality, when there are children in the house,

life goes on in the most humdrum way with face-washings and feedings and lessons and puttings-to-bed; and in the very moment when, perhaps, behind a locked door two adults are facing each other in final despair, at the nursery table someone is poking a spoonful of applesauce into a small, innocent face.

Therefore the statement I made on the first page of this book: that *The Son of Adam Wyngate* was the portrayal of a drama seen through the foreground action of six dancing figures.

In the main, the critics have justified my decision, many of them stating that the children were the best of the book. A school principal said, "No other author in the country is writing about children as excitingly as this." From California came a letter from my friend Rufus particularly praising the children. "They are in the way all through the book—just as they are in real life! A masterpiece!"

But there were dissenting opinions. A neighbor said the children "got in the way" to such an extent that it interfered with his interest in the story. "I'd have killed that little Jennifer. . . ."

Even Aroldo, who is a warm admirer of my skill as a craftsman, frowned dubiously and said, "Yes—it is the classical method of the Italian 'masque'—the comedians who come tumbling onto the stage when the drama gives out or gets too melo. But. . . ." Too much, he thinks. Too much of the children.

There was much for me to write now. Not, as yet, the story, for I still did not know what that was to be, but I knew the world in which it would take place. Brooklyn

[54]

in the early 1900's. This world, with all its places, houses, streets, rooms, churches, vistas, was to be inhabited by large numbers of people whom I must create; some of them in detail and at length, and most vividly, for they were important foreground characters who would move the plot; others more briefly and less vividly, for they were merely to be glimpsed as they went about their business.

First of all, there were the names to get. It is hard to think about people and impossible to talk about them until they are named. I do not know why this should be so difficult that I can think of no word for it but agonizing. I worried at their names awake and asleep, driving, resting, eating, visiting. For days or weeks I would struggle with one single character rightly to name him, actually a sort of mad seizure, shaking him by the throat—Tell me! Tell me! You must tell me! What's your name? Your real name?

Eventually he gets a name that will stick. When they are wrongly named, there is no peace for any of us. In Genesis, after all, it is stated that Adam was given the task of finding names for every created thing—which can be taken as a measure of its importance. For me at least the naming—right naming—is part of the very structure of the character. With the wrong name, the character looks wrong, talks wrong, does the wrong things.

I named my hero Samuel and named him wrong.

His wife was Louise; his children, Joyce, Cecil, Sara, Jennifer, Cherry, and Runo; his elder brother, Ramsey; sister, Edith; his associate, Justin Hughes; his father, Adam Wyngate.

They were at first just wraiths of characters, for I did

not yet know what they had to do. All except Samuel were rightly named.

To my grief and endless trouble, Samuel was named wrong.

With all this teeming in my mind, I now became afflicted with that plague of writers, procrastination. Almost any activity seemed preferable to sitting down at the typewriter and getting started. I made excuses, sought alibis, dashed about the countryside in my car, went visiting, made daily appointments; particularly did I spend hours surpervising the work going on at my house, or hunting for old mantels, doors, or paneling, in antique shops.

A good deal of time passed.

My heart grew heavy with dread, for it really seemed that I would never be able to make myself write this book.

Then, fortunately, I got one of my terrible colds.

Nine

THERE IS nothing to do but give up, obey the doctor, take the medicine, oil on chest, compress around throat, inhale steam, bedrest, windows open or closed as the opinion of the moment commands, either food or fast, ice pack or heat, or both.

It is all so boring that to forget about it and plunge into a make-believe world is a blessed escape. So there I was at last at the typewriter.

Some writers can write a story in chronological sequence from birth onward. It has never been my way, perhaps because my first professional work was dramatic, namely, for the screen. I construct a novel as if for drama, organizing the material so that there are a certain number of Acts with definite Curtains (or Fades); and before each curtain a carefully prepared for and delivered Climax.

The word climax is frequently used in ordinary conversation. As, the climax of a long illness; or strain. And it is correctly understood to mean the culmination of a sustained conflict during which the opposing forces are interlocked like two wrestlers struggling for the ascendancy. These opposing forces can be anything. Good against evil. Life against death. Hope against dread. Age against youth. Success against failure. Pleasure against pain. Or, as in my book, love against hate.

And the climaxes can be either stupendous or trifling—catching the train; meeting the friend; getting the X-ray report; as well as the lightning stroke, or the bullet, or the judge's gavel.

Small or large, they happen every day. Life is made up of them. We see things happen to people, but usually do not see the beginnings, or the meanings, the final effects. There is too much going on; too many rings to the circus.

This is the artist's opportunity. He can close down those other rings and focus attention on the one where he is putting on his particular drama.

Literature reflects life, it is said. But it can do more. It can reveal what life usually keeps hidden—the beginnings, the ends, and the meanings.

The artist can turn any event of life, small or large, into an important climax if he wishes. The trick is the use of emphasis. By emphasis (the spotlight) he can carve out and hold up to notice the sustained conflict between opposing forces that goes before the climax; then isolate the action that delivers the final blow. Then he can attach significance to the whole episode and so make his point.

If he is a good craftsman, the art of his arrangements will be invisible; and his work will be judged "real," and "convincing." If not, the machinery will be apparent; and the work will be judged "contrived."

I have said that before I begin a book I must know the problem, which is to say, the opposing forces, in this case, love and hate; and must know the solution, namely, which of those forces is to conquer (love is to conquer hate); and that quite often I write, at the very outset, the final scene or scenes that show how the protagonists of the opposing forces resolve their enmity.

But this does not mean that I know the exact event that brings the conflict to an end, for it could be anything—a burst of tears; a sneeze; the accidental slamming of a door; or the ringing of the dinner bell—and you will not know until you come to the actual writing of the scene in context which one will be best. You will try a dozen or more. Something inconsequential, even trifling, is quite likely to be the most effective, for the size of a climax is not made by that final event but by the length of time and amount of force engaged in the struggle that leads up to it.

In this particular story, since I did not intend to end it with the permanent breakup of the Wyngate family, I made sure that Samuel and Louise could eventually resolve their enmity in a credible manner by writing, long in advance, several scenes of the two of them talking out, in a quiet way, their differences; and so achieving at least a partial reconciliation. These scenes showed that these particular people could face what had happened to them, pick up the pieces, and go on together. And so the book would not end like that movie of the two lost in the arctic snow, going on through eternity shrieking each other's names.

In a novel of any size, there is more than one climax. A novel with only one climax would be comparable to a one-act play. In this novel of mine there were seven climaxes, mounting in intensity to the last.

The decision, in advance, as to how many acts there will be in your play, or climaxes in your novel, is something that can drive you crazy. How shall you know? I find myself waving my hand in the air in long curves, chanting off, as my hand rises and falls: Here he worries—here he fears—here he doubts—here he suspects—here he knows part—here he knows all—here he goes to pieces.

These are all climaxes. A series of them. And even though it seems like a surf rider tossed whichever way the waves happen to come, yet it makes a sort of sense; it makes a crescendo; and you begin to feel a rhythm and a gathering tension. After many efforts, many experiments and failures, you begin to catch the beat. You both create it and obey it. And as you write, your writing follows it, at first vaguely and fumblingly; then more firmly; and at last with confidence and precision.

You find then, those exact scenes that show:

1) his worry.
2) his fear.
3) his doubt.
4) his suspicion.
5) his partial discovery.
6) his complete discovery.
7) his collapse.

Though much effective writing can be done by instinct, I do not see how good dramatic writing, whether for stage or screen or fiction, can be produced without the author's having the technique of pace-making. This grows out of the knowledge that, if there is such a thing as a climax, then there must be the leading up to it and the retreat from it. For a book cannot be *all* climaxes; nor a play.

This makes the three kinds of writing, preparatory, climactic, and winding up.

If you were reciting the story aloud, as the minstrel tells his tale, you would find that you would be using a different voice for these three kinds of action. Every child knows when his mother is getting ready to say, "And they lived happily ever after." And if you are writing the story instead of telling it, you must do the same thing. You must indicate which of the three kinds of action you are describing by the pace of it, the kind of sentences used, by punctuation, and English and composition.

A book (and music too, and the dance) unfolds in the dimension of *time*. It is not all there before you in a single instant as a painting or piece of sculpture or a building is. So we say (as we could not say of a painting) it has *parts in time,* namely, a beginning and a middle and an end.

In a musical composition, directions for finding your way through the dimension of time are given. The *tempi* (the different speeds) are designated by the composer at the beginning. Also, the length of the whole piece is measured and the parts composed in relation to the whole. There are so many "bars" (or principal beats) or measures. There are parts, or movements, comparable to the acts of a play. Also there are the same three types of material, preparatory, climactic, and winding up.

The expert dramatic writer (or composer) will never put climactic writing in a preparatory section or vice versa. Nor waste on a winding-up section the detailed descriptions or analyses of a preparatory section.

Preparatory writing is slow, detailed, very close in to the characters (since we are searching out motives and first causes); it covers much paper; usually comprises scenes, descriptions, dialogues, author-narrative, thought-streams.

Climactic writing is also very close in, but swift; concentrated; short. Here we are dealing with results; no time for analysis now; and if anyone is in the way he will be run over. This type of action is set forth in factual, unadorned sentences; it is not the place to use a figure of speech; it is most often a single scene that does not cover a great deal of paper.

Winding-up writing is also short, but it is not close in to the characters or situations. The author is moving away from them, depicting wide sweeps of action and time on a falling cadence—they lived happily ever after.

As an author writes, he knows if it is preparatory, or climactic or winding-up writing that he is doing. He had better know it. If he doesn't, he can turn out fearfully dull pages; bewildering, too.

The heartbreaking and backbreaking aspect of this is that climaxes are variables; they shift and change as the writing progresses. What was a climax some weeks ago no longer is—something has topped it.

And for the sake of the power of the book you must let them remain variables. Let them move forward or back; let them vibrate until at last the movement ceases and the climax has found its place in time, properly related to all that goes before and comes after.

It is, of course, the author who is making the climaxes, and making them shift. He does this by shifting the emphasis. Emphasis is the tool that is constantly in the artist's hand. And whenever a climax is shifted, then there must be a complete rewrite, for what was climactic has become preparatory and must be rewritten as such with a vast deal of new material added; a new climax must be invented; and the wind-up will be in a different place, on a different page, differently written.

This dramatic style of writing avoids monotony by giving the whole book a changing pace; style, too; actually a rhythmic pattern. Many books are so lacking in rhythm, it is as if a speaker tells a tale all on one note without a single inflection or change of pace or expression. It can kill the best story.

But plays, they say, are not written; they are rewritten. And it is the same with the dramatic novel. There is bound to be endless juggling of climaxes and curtains, and the whole thing is written over many times.

Ten

IN THE BIBLICAL story of creation, chaos came before shapes and forms.

That winter I made the chaos. And it was huge. I could have made a dozen novels out of it. An overabundance of incidents and characters and episodes, indeed, life stories for every character, plus an exact visual portrait. They got talking in their scenes; pages of dialogue; scenes done both briefly and at exhaustive length.

From day to day I could not remember what I had written and filed away the day before. But I knew that my invented world was growing in richness, reality, and interest. My characters were beginning to be companions to me, quite exciting companions. Each one would have made a book. Indeed I found it difficult to keep them in any sort of proportion to my main line, particularly as the main line was not yet clear, except as a general theme.

It was a veritable jungle. Through that jungle there must, eventually, wind a little path—and that would be the story line.

The path must come out of the jungle at exactly the

right place. And that would be the point of the whole book, the delivery of my message, determined long ago on U.S. 30.

And the path, in its windings, must take in certain vistas—points of interest; and those would be the climaxes.

I feared that, after all the labor, I would never find this path through the jungle. I knew better; but it was such unremitting nervous anxiety that, had it been expressed vocally, it would have been a thin moan—rising and falling but never ceasing. I began to wake earlier, to sleep less soundly and less long.

Mary to Mary . . . how can you take a single step, logically, until you know where you are going? Which means, how can you begin a book until you have ended it? You can't. But how can you write the ending except as the culmination of all the steps that have gone before? You can't. So you have to write the whole thing at once. . . .

What's your book about, Mary?

About this clergyman . . . a wonderful man really . . . *really* wonderful, a man you have to love . . . very human and attractive, nothing weak or sentimental about him . . . he has a big city parish, but he's a mystic too. . . . Ah, yes . . . I could call it a study of sacred and profane love. . . .

Now . . . suddenly . . . I can write the thumbnail synopsis. A study of sacred and profane love. Samuel Wyngate, mystic; that portion of his life which comprises his trial and emergence. (The death and rebirth theme.) He is an Interior Soul. Unsuited to large city parish and family responsibilities. Great and jealous love of Louise, his charming and flighty wife. He is being crushed and borne down, but could stand up under it except for his weak point—excessive love of his wife. Story focuses on Ramsey, his older brother with whom

[65]

Louise has had an affair. She has had others too. When Samuel discovers in himself hatred first for Ramsey, then Louise, he goes to pieces. Can no longer take Communion, administer the Sacrament, preach, or keep his church.

I pinned this paragraph up on my bulletin board. It was the beginning of a definite story, though it suggested many different angles. Was this going to be a Cain and Abel story? Or a diatribe against worldliness? Or plea for the celibacy of the clergy? Or all of them?

I wondered how other people would like this Brooklyn world I was bringing to life, and the characters, and the questions that were raised and discussed. I wanted to talk to someone about it.

The public has the concept of an author standing on a pinnacle of power, turning a deaf ear to anyone who would suggest that he change even so much as one word for another.

But this is far from the case. The extent to which editors and publishers influence the output of their authors is astounding; witness the controversy of the last year in the *Saturday Review of Literature* between those who believed that Maxwell Perkins, editor, killed his author, Thomas Wolfe; and those who believe that the author killed the editor.

A writer writes for a wide public. To talk or write even to a hundred people is airing one's thoughts widely, and in the end it may turn out to be millions.

The public will tell you what it thinks of your work. It will write you many letters. But by then it's too late to pay attention to what they say.

Before that, the critics will tell you. These are trained men and women occupying positions of strategic importance. And by then, it's too late to pay any attention to what they say either.

Before that, the editorial board of the publishing firm will have told you.

Mark Haverford once said that every one of the board, perhaps three persons or five or any number, studies the manuscript and writes an opinion on it. Then they meet and discuss it. They are obliged, before sending any word to the author, to come to agreement. If there is a controversial point, they thresh it out, decide what to say, then pass the word to the author.

For instance, in *Green Grass of Wyoming,* they told me my young lovers were too passionate and my man too profane. I did not see it, but every member of the board was against me. So I agreed to modify the passionateness of the youngsters but not the profanity of the man. A western rancher simply could not watch his priceless wild stallion leap over the impassable barrier that had been built at great cost to catch and contain him, and exclaim, "Gee Whitacker!"

Besides, there was plenty of swearing in *My Friend Flicka* and not even my Catholic nun fans (the most enthusiastic of all my readers) had ever objected.

Even before the editorial board of the publishing firm has had its say about a manuscript, there have been consultants and critics of an informal kind; a best friend, a member of the family, a neighbor. By such talks an author can discover for instance if his hero is liked or not; if some

[67]

episode can be believed or if it strains credulity; if any secondary character is stealing the spotlight.

All of this is a great help, so it's best to listen to what people have to say about your book before it's too late. But there's a danger in this. You have to know where to stand firm. It's possible to get harm rather than help. It really requires a technique to sift the good from the bad advice. What you want is an emotional reaction, like Russ's "I wish it was me!" and never a critical opinion, which is of value only if it comes from a trained mind, trained in story values.

Back in the years when I wrote for the screen, we liked to get an audience reaction before the picture was shown to the public. I remember once when Mr. Ingram, my director, called in the little office boy, Pat, and showed him a comedy scene in our private projection room. (Movie audiences, it was supposed, averaged about twelve years of mental age.)

Pat laughed uproariously. Then Mr. Ingram made a mistake. He said, "You think that's a good comedy scene, Pat? Think I should leave it in the picture?"

Pat couldn't answer. Ingram forced him. Pat squirmed, at last said, "Well, to tell the truth, Mr. Ingram, no, I don't think you should leave it in."

"But you laughed at it. You must have thought it was funny."

"Well, *I* thought it was funny, but I don't think other people will think so."

"You think I should take it out then?"

"Yes, I do."

This is the kind of nonsense you run into if you invite

or even allow critical opinions from those who cannot be expected to have them.

Screen writers are cursed with amateur criticism. They are obliged to submit their copy to the examination of so many people, most of them ignorant, and all with different ideas, that it amounts to a sort of enforced collaboration. Most movie scripts are, thus, written by a gang. In my case, this precluded any possibility of doing my best work and is the principal reason I gave up screen writing.

The author of a novel can sit alone and secure in his little room. He need never expose his pages to an outside eye unless he wishes. If he does wish, then let him remember the difference between an emotional reaction, which anyone can have, and a critical opinion, which only an expert can have. And even an expert has his own prejudices; he may always want the sentimental; or the conventional; or he may be governed by copybook rules.

My habit is to invite discussion only when I myself feel it will be a help, or at least harmless. And I am careful whose criticism I take. I guard my idea, my point of view, and my characters against change or damage. I listen to everything, but hold the line for my book as I see it. Accept correction if in my deepest heart I agree—not otherwise.

And I have it in my contract that no changes can be made without my consent. After all, it is I who sign the book and will be held responsible for every word in it.

The time having now come when I wanted to talk about my work, I thought of Whit Burnett.

Usually an author has one particular consultant on the

editorial board of the publishing firm. But my consultant was Whit Burnett, who had in the first place made the connection between me and Lippincott. Though not a Lippincott editor, he had a business arrangement with them by which authors introduced by him would, if published, carry the Story Press imprint on their books. All my books had been Story Press books.

Whit, moreover, had been my teacher for that one six-week session. He understood my aims and methods, and I understood him too, and was not in the least put off by his far-famed explosiveness. Hallie (his wife) still reminds me that I once said, "I don't mind Whit." I can say much more than that. I respect his artistic conscience, his knowledge, his outstanding achievements, and I am always on the alert for the occasional lightning flash through his thunderings.

But Whit had now left Lippincott and gone to Dutton's.

During one of those luncheon-table discussions between author and publisher that are such a pleasant feature of a literary career, I was asked how I felt about losing my consultant. I said I regretted it.

Knowing or at least surmising that Whit had been wafting Lorelei songs in my direction, they asked if I intended leaving them to follow Whit to Dutton's.

Being uprooted is painful to me. I am just naturally faithful if not actually clinging. So I said, No, I would stay with them.

A few weeks later Mark Haverford wrote me that they had retained Whit as special editor for me at a fee of one thousand dollars. He would hold himself in readiness to discuss the story I was at work on any time I wanted. When the book was finished he would edit it.

So now I made an appointment with Whit Burnett and ran down to New York to see him.

Eleven

WHIT BURNETT, in spite of his knowledge and experience and critical and professional powers, has never lost his ability to react. He can enthuse, vituperate, throw his hat in the air, glower.

I think I really value this in him more than anything else. Most of his opinions (though not all) I can arrive at myself if I take time enough, thought enough, and am sufficiently objective. But, like the majority of writers, doubt and pessimism ride me; and Whit's sudden, soaring enthusiasms go far beyond what I could ever feel myself, and thus give me support.

If, now, in this impending conference, I should show him enough of what I had written to be a sample, I might get from him a favorable reaction as I had got one from Russ. I might get more—a favorable critical opinion, and from Whit that would mean something. If it was not favorable, I could profit from that too. But I was sure it would be favorable. Whit is too wise to discourage an author before she has really shown what she intends to do with her subject.

But how could I show it to him or describe it to him when it was still just chaos? I wanted him, as it were, to taste it. I would just give him some good mouthfuls of my chaos so that he could chew it and get the full flavor. I would give him my exposition.

Someone has written that if the world were being freshly created, its past must be created with it. There must be not only the horse and wagon but hoofprints and wheel ruts from previous journeys.

Wherever I begin my story, even if I begin it at the moment when Samuel discovers his wife's infidelity, I must also write out the full past of my principal characters from birth onward, namely, the exposition.

I had written it. This had been evolved, as a matter of course, when I brought into being that world which was to be the background of my story.

In the novels of Sir Walter Scott the exposition usually fills the whole of Chapter Two, many pages packed with such long paragraphs a reader groans at sight of it.

Fortunately, present-day writing forbids this. New techniques have been found that spare the reader such painful labor. You can begin at the end and tell the whole story in a series of flashbacks; or mingle the past with the present as you go along.

At the time I was writing *My Friend Flicka* Whit told me of an author who was obliged to cut a hundred and fifty pages from the early part of the book. All "author-narrative—wonderful stuff really; but she used it all later. Not in a solid chunk but just trickling it through, you know. . . ."

[73]

A neat label—the "trickle through."

My exposition was thirty pages long. It covered a couple of generations and created a substantial background for the present drama, as follows:

The Wyngate family has, for generations, given its sons to the Episcopalian ministry. The family homestead is "Marshlands" at Kennebunkport, Maine.

Late in the last century Adam Wyngate was the head of the family. Though a man of brilliant gifts, he had always chosen to keep a little country parish and pursue his studies in quiet as he plowed the fields of his farm. He and his beautiful southern wife, Charlotte Ramsey, had three children: Ramsey, Edith and, considerably younger, Samuel, who was destined, almost from birth, to follow in his father's footsteps.

Kennebunkport was a summer resort as well as seaport; and when, one summer, the little blonde girl, Louise, came there with her mother, Samuel, now thirteen, fell in love with her. His older brother Ramsey, of college age, amused himself by bullying and tormenting his little brother, and found the best way to do this was to fascinate Louise, and attach her to himself. Thus the pattern was set that, thirty years later, was to shake the structure of Samuel's worldly career to the very foundations.

As Louise grew to young womanhood, she was surrounded by suitors, for she had an irresistible feminine seductiveness. But Ramsey was the favored one; and it was taken for granted that they would be married. Ramsey, however, had a calculating eye to the future, and suddenly became engaged to the homely but wealthy Anna Gillespie of Boston. They were married and went abroad to live, thus leaving the field clear for Samuel.

Charlotte, meanwhile, has died. And there comes the tragic accident by which Adam loses both legs. Samuel, recently ordained for the ministry, takes over his father's parish at Kennebunkport, and receives from him also, during the year or two that Adam lingers before dying, intensive instruction in psychology and mysticism.

After Adam's death, Samuel and Louise are married. The spiritual bent of the young man, already strong, becomes firmly established. Though intensely happy in a human way with his long desired wife and the children that come rapidly one after the other, he finds his heart constantly seeking the atmosphere of that boundless world of ecstatic love that is the only possible home for the true mystic.

He prospers. He has personal charm, powers of oratory, natural leadership; and when, through his sister Edith, he receives a call to St. Stephen's, an important parish in Brooklyn Heights, he moves there with his family. Edith is already living there, the wealthy widow of Herbert Clark.

Marshlands is now owned by Ramsey, Edith, and Samuel in equal shares, and the two last always spend their summers there.

At this point, I thought, the actual story would begin; with Samuel forty-two, Louise forty, Ramsey and Edith about ten years older.

If Whit read this, he would get the taste of the book that I wanted him to have. I could also show him a few of the scattered scenes I had written.

Twelve

THE MEETING between Whit and me took place at my brother's apartment in New York.

Whit arrived, very poker-faced, hurried, and business-like. We stood talking a moment. I recounted what I had been doing and where I had got to, then handed him the sheets of paper, showed him to another room, and left him alone.

Talks with such a writer as I am must be very difficult for an editor. Whit once said to me, "The trouble in being your editor is that you not only write your book, you write your way to your book by writing several other books first."

There is truth in this. I do frequently shift my angle of vision; as if a painter should set up his easel in several different places, take fresh canvas for each shift, and paint the whole thing over.

There was hardly a page or sentence that I presented to Whit that day that would be in the finished work, and I knew it. He could hardly know it. He came out of the room saying, "Adam is your best character."

Now this was impossible, for Samuel must be the best character. This exposition, of course, dealt with beginnings primarily; and Adam was merely the beginning of Samuel, so I was disconcerted. Wait—just wait till I really got to Samuel! (But why had he not been taken with Samuel? Even those small sketches and scenes of him?) This was the beginning of my worry about Samuel.

Whit said, "This is just notes, you know—a whole book of notes."

I said, "I know."

He then began to catch at and admire the bits of actual scenes, the little boy walking behind Adam as he plowed; the evening duet between Samuel and Louise in the early days of their marriage; Jennifer in church, looking at her father in the pulpit and wondering if he could be called a handsome man.

"And a very good idea here, the clergyman's clinic, which is the rage today under the label of psychosomatic medicine. But as you point out, there's nothing new about it. Christ said, 'Take up thy bed and walk.' . . ."

He questioned me with impatience as to what the story was? I really did not yet know. I tried to outline a path—one of the many possible paths—that entered that jungle. But I had to fall back on my abstract of the book: that the conflict was between Samuel's love of God and love of his wife—the question being, which one really commanded him? And that when Ramsey and Anna returned from abroad to live once again in this country and spend their summers with the rest of them at Marshlands, it became apparent which one has command over him; for he finds himself full of the negative emotions—worry, fear, doubt, jealousy, hatred. These increase to the climax.

"And what's the climax?" demanded Whit.

But I was far from being ready with that. There were too many ways he could break down. "Samuel goes to pieces in some way."

I thought then and still think that Whit minimizes the importance of an abstract, and feels that an author can begin immediately with scenes and story line. But this is the opposite of the truth with me. The story is so easy that I hold off on it as long as I can, dealing exhaustively with those elements that are underneath; testing the abstractions at every step, for it is they which, in the last analysis, will provide the meaning and the truth of all that is to come, and the whole weight and authority of the book.

Scenes emerge of themselves when the proper foundations have been laid, like the froth that springs out on the top of a racing comber. First the deep waters underneath; then life and movement, the ground swells and the wind.

Scenes, moreover, are actually dangerous. When you move a human being through a scene, saying, "He did—" and "He said—" you'd better be telling the truth or it's a calumny; and your character, and therefore your story, will suffer from it. But, right or wrong, once they are on paper they hypnotize you and everyone else. No one will let you give them up.

Whit and I lunched together in a nearby restaurant. I did try to describe a few of the scenes I had tentatively sketched, such as the little girl singing the solo in the choir, and a few others. He muttered, "Marvelous—marvelous material." He was intrigued, I saw, by the "taste" of my chaos, which I had given him, and went on talking about it. He talked more than I, his own mind filling out the empty spots and going off in directions that I would never take.

This is one of the disadvantages of talking about your story before you've really got it to jell. Someone else wants to make it jell. Sometimes they succeed. You have to be on your guard.

I got back to Monroe wound up several notches tighter. I was elated. My world and characters had been presented to another human being and had stood up under scrutiny. This proved they had backbone.

Whit had shown genuine enthusiasm. Though this was terribly important for me, yet it had its dangers. I hoped I had not oversold myself, but feared that I had. Ideas thrown out tentatively, which I hardly as yet had confidence in myself, had taken him by storm. And then *his* reaction had rebounded on me and sold *me* when it wasn't yet time for me to be sold. The decision as to what must and must not go into the book must be made in a far cooler and more judicial mood than this. All thin, thin ice under me as yet. . . .

But why had he not liked my hero even a little? What was it that his voice and the turn of his head had expressed? Was it contempt?

He had actually been sympathetic with Louise and her infidelity, almost as if he said, Well, after all, a clergyman —what could you expect?

I saw that here, in the very inception of the story, this danger lay hidden. I had never dreamed of such a thing.

[80]

Perhaps a large section of the public would consider that any clergyman would be emasculated by his calling; or that no real man—only as it were half a man—would choose such a calling.

This was an appalling difficulty. I didn't know how I was going to meet it, for I would be dealing with preconceived opinions on the part of the reading public. But it had to be met and overcome. Samuel himself must overcome it.

Well . . . go ahead; flounder and slither along; keep all the windows open; drift with every wind that blows; write . . . write . . . write. . . .

Thirteen

SOON AFTER my visit with Whit I lunched with the Haverfords (Leigh Bradley now made the third) and garnered some more thoughts—perhaps I should say worries—about my hero.

In most books that have a clergyman hero or character, his actual sermons are not part of the book. When he gets into the pulpit the chapter ends. Or the sermon may be referred to as "moving" or "strong" or whatever. But it seemed to me that what a clergyman would say in the pulpit would express in the most ordered form the essence of his thinking and living. I decided his sermons ought to be in the book.

There were also his hours of preparation. When did he do that work? In his study at home? Or the church? In the middle of the night? And from what sprang his ideas and inspirations? Did he have the proverbial barrel and, when he had exhausted his supply of sermons, turn the barrel over and begin again? (Not my preacher . . .)

"But it's not going to be all sermons, is it?" hoped Leigh.

I reassured them. "It's about love. Sacred and profane love. It could be called that."

"It's been used."

"I know. How would you like *Man of God?*"

They did not care for it. It was too limiting. They preferred *The Son of Adam Wyngate*. And so did I, though none of us was completely satisfied with it.

Underneath our talk I had feelers out, probing. I was writing a book about religion with a clergyman as hero. These men would pass on it. Did they ever think about such things? Were they at all interested, really?

As we discussed the sermons, their faces were solemn and respectful. No one was going to make a break. But I suddenly realized they were talking about my Samuel as if he was of a breed unknown to them. And so he was, considered as a clergyman; but, considered as a man, Samuel must be known and judged as any man can be, as Mark and Frank and Leigh themselves can be. I must never make him so much the man of God that he ceases to be a man.

They were not judging him as a man; they were judging him as a queer specimen. They were not drawn to him in the least.

Here it was again!

I felt a sort of panic. All—*all* depended on the power of this character to draw readers to him.

When I returned to Monroe, all my thought was concentrated on this.

The sermons, I decided, would help a great deal. His inmost thoughts, his hope and his heart, his faith in God and love for men—all this could be disclosed in his sermons, in his talks with those who came to consult him, in his discussions with his friend Quentin Gerrity, and in his hours of solitary reflection. Work on these things.

All winter I worked at it. Samuel's thought. It grew into thick essays; sermons; conversations. I ransacked my file for the notes on religious thought that I had been accumulating for twenty years. Out of these could come my Samuel, the man who could change the feeling of a room merely by walking through it, who could sweep away despair and pour in hope like a floodlight. . . . *"Lift up your heads, O ye gates!"*

The writing of a novel takes possession of an author's life and commands it, imposing hours, a rhythm, demanding sacrifices of all else. This is servitude, but agreeable, cleansing the conscience, banishing idleness and boredom; giving the final answer to *cui bono?* When I am between novels, there begins to be again a faint restlessness and guilt.

I am an early riser. In childhood I learned the magic of the sunrise hours and the empty, silent world in which no one is awake but herdsmen and fishermen, milkmaids and the birds.

In the Swiss Tyrol, when I was eleven, my sisters and I would rise at three or four and climb mountains, returning at nine for an enormous breakfast of which I particularly remember the hot corn muffins drenched in butter and honey, and huge pitchers of milk.

When I am writing, these early hours hold and nurture my best work. I can suddenly leave the typewriter, go to the window or out the door, and stand there, endless refreshment pouring into me.

At the beginning of the writing I am content to rise at six or five thirty, make that first cup of strong, delicious coffee, slick hair, wash face, and begin work. But as the tension increases, I rise earlier and earlier. Toward the end I am doing well if I can sleep from ten until one or two. Then, through the day, I fall asleep at odd moments; waiting for a parcel to be wrapped in a store; while gasoline is being put in my car; waiting my turn in an office; sometimes, holding the receiver to my ear, waiting for a call to be put through.

At noon or one o'clock my work is done for the day. It would be easy then to drop on the bed, but if I did I should not rise again, no, not all day. I've tried it. And it deprives me of any good, sound, nighttime sleep; for by that time I'm half slept out, my mind is active again, and sleep is a wretched, shallow tossing and listening to the clock, or turning the bedside light on to scribble notes.

What I do like to do when work is done is take out my car and, slowly, drive. Just drift about on the lovely country roads. It is best to be alone, for I am too tired for speech. I am gradually withdrawing my mind from that far world where it has, for many hours, been occupied. I am trying to make it look outward again, instead of inward. I hardly know where I am or what I am looking at. My eyes are so altered by the continual inner looking that they cannot discern a single clear outline. Everything is covered with a haze.

Gradually my sight comes back. I question myself as I pass the beautiful trees of the roadside, Is that a maple?

A tulip? An oak? Beech? And I look particularly at the shapes of individual leaves.

It is a simple exercise. But I really doubt if my eyesight would have held up without damage during the writing of that book without it.

After an hour or two of this, I can again see; I can speak; I can give a sensible order in the shops.

When even a single chapter has been written with numbered pages, a momentum is created. When the thing won't move, just read it through and it carries on of itself a little further. Then do it again. As it gets bulky it generates a powerful drive forward.

But though, in that winter of 1949, I fell into my usual writing habits and kept regular hours, I could not yet write the first chapter. The folder labeled "Sermons" grew thick. I wrote more than I could ever use. The best of them went into the finished book.

Fourteen

EARLY THAT summer of 1949 my brother asked me to go sailing with him over the Fourth of July weekend.

His boat is a thirty-five-foot cutter called the *Tinavire* from the French song *"P'tit Navire."* In the spring and early summer he keeps it at the yacht club at Oyster Bay and goes out weekends. For his midsummer vacation he sails it up to Cape Cod. Or should I say down? Yes, Down East, down the wind. . . .

He had a summer cottage at the end of the Cape, Wellfleet, and back of it a pathless, fragrant, salty, sandy, windy woods (in which I promptly got lost).

I went to New York the night before, and in the morning we took the train to Oyster Bay, then a taxi to the club, then the launch out to the anchored boat.

We sailed the Sound to Port Jefferson, where we had a rendezvous with Seth Hart in his boat, the *Ariadne.*

We joined his party for cocktails, then back in our dinghy to the *Tinavire,* and into our bathing suits and overboard.

I did not stop to think that it was three years since I

"Why nothing, Reese—she is simply that sort. There are lots of such women. It's a fairly common type, in fact a classic type."

But common or not, she was intriguing to Reese. (As she proved to be to Whit. Whit was to say in his report on the book when it was finished, "The interest in Louise and curiosity as to what has made her the way she is, is so handled by the author that it acquires the suspense of a detective story.")

It is true that in my handling of Louise I kept her mysterious and unexplained, but not for the reason Whit mentioned.

Whit accepts far more of the conclusions of modern psychology than I can. Considering Louise as a "case" and "abnormal" (as he did), therefore neurotic and possibly psychotic, then there must be something of importance that started her on the downward path; and to hold this important something back, and then near the end, disclose it, is a dramatic device on the part of the author.

The scene in the book in which this disclosure is finally made was as follows. Edith asks Louise, "What's the matter with you anyway Louise? How could you do such things?" And in reply Louise gives the account of the way she had started (or been started) by the impassioned kisses of an older man when she was a little thing of six or seven. She adds, "Some girls are never virgin, Edith."

Whit never thought I made enough of this scene, the climax of the mystery. But it was not a climax to me. I did not deliver it in climactic writing. I did not prepare for it as a climax, or put it in the place in the story that it would have had, had it been a climax. As a matter of fact, it did not, to me, have enough weight or body to be a climax because it was too ordinary. (I remember a girl telling me she had always wondered, as a child, why her uncle closed his eyes when he kissed her.)

There is the term "woman's intuition." If it is true that intuition belongs to women rather than men, then this surprising masculine dependence on psychoanalysis can be understood.

Perhaps Louise, today, would be psychoanalyzed. They would find out what every old aunty knows; that, yes, no doubt something started her off on the wrong tack; she had bad luck; there were unfortunate influences; and her erotic nature was too much aroused, too early and too constantly. But making allowance for all that, Louise was what she was as a blonde is a blonde; and she would not change unless she got thoroughly frightened; or physically incapacitated; or an awakened conscience. She simply liked variety. Perhaps she liked the excitement of the chase. Is there anyone who imagines that it is entirely natural for either men or women to be monogamous?

Now that I have denied any intention to make a detective story out of Louise I must explain why I did make her a mystery—carefully, purposely, and at great pains.

This was because she was the villain of the book.

Since those whom we understand we cannot help loving or liking at least a little, and since I did not want my readers to like her much, I tried to prevent them from understanding her. So, as I drew her scenes, I showed what she did, how she looked, what she said—but never what was in her heart or mind.

I even tried to keep from genuine understanding of her

myself; wrote her down as an obvious type and let it go at that.

But that night spent with Reese on the deck of the *Tinavire* put an end to any mystery Louise might have for me. I knew her inside and out.

We discussed every possible angle of her character. The double standard. Are men and women the same? Could she be an immoral woman and yet a good mother? Could she ever have got away with it, being in so high a place with the eyes of the congregation upon her? What were her virtues? Why did Samuel love her so desperately? Did she love him back? Or did she really love Ramsey? Or no one but herself and her own loveliness? And what about the children? Were they all Samuel's? Or was there a cuckoo in the nest? If so, which one? Who was the father? Did Samuel know or suspect? If he did, what was his attitude about this?

I saw that the answering of all these questions was going to provide me with a mass of interesing plot material.

My opinion about Louise did not change. I continued to consider her a fairly common type. There have always been sirens from the time of Lilith onward. Early in this century the word "vamp" came in. And Mrs. Eddy's term, "animal magnetism."

When my book finally came out the character of Louise was much discussed.

Dot Gossler said, "We all know Louise. She's all around us. And she won't change. She'll go right on till she's about fifty, maybe fifty-five. . . ."

And when women got together, talking the book over,

[92]

there were often reminiscences beginning with the words, "I knew a woman once who . . ." The conversation would end up on the topic of sex appeal. What was it anyway? Actually no one knew. I don't know either.

Sterling North said in his review in the *New York World-Telegram*, "After about the twelfth lover I think her husband should have put his foot down."

Fifteen

IT IS A critical matter for Kim when anyone talks to me, especially a man. Even more than the sex he objects to the symbol—the trousers. His back hair will bristle at sight of blue jeans at our door even with a woman in them.

Another hazard is a gate or doorway.

One day that summer Reese came to Monroe; we were going to drive up to Wellfleet in my car.

We met at the gate of the white picket fence that surrounds the front yard of the Masons' house, and I carefully stood between Reese and Kim; for here were all the dangers together: trousers, a stranger who kissed me, and a gate.

But Reese is tall, and looked over my head. "That's a fine dog!" He pushed me aside. "What a head!" He took that broad-browed head strongly between his two hands.

The look of astonishment on Kim's face was laughable. He instantly capitulated. From that moment on he accepted Reese, looking at me almost sheepishly, faintly smiling, faintly ashamed.

Driving to Cape Cod, Kim went with us. He had the

tonneau to himself as usual, the dishpan for his feedings on the floor, with cans of Pard, can opener, bag of ground meal.

Reese and I amused ourselves.

No detour was too long if it would take us to good fresh lobster.

We talked of books, Pearl Buck's *Of Men and Women.* We talked, it follows, of love. The Sunday paper had come out with a list of the ten best novels of all time. One of them was *Madame Bovary,* and Reese had not read it. I told him the tale. How it was called a great love story, but the real theme of it was how love can be destructive, how it can be like a drug, consuming and devouring all other interests; duties even; and ethics, or the merest decency.

From that we got to Louise . . . and Louise . . . and Louise. . . .

I had been writing a good deal about her since that night on the *Tinavire,* and I was finding it difficult to continue playing her entirely from the outside.

It is habitual with me to enter into the hearts and minds of my characters. So much so that an English critic was to make the amusing comment: "They are well drawn —not to say drawn and quartered." Since the same critic said the book was "terribly exciting," I flattered myself it might be a good idea to draw and quarter your characters.

I had now thought so much about Louise that, as I feared, I was getting to like her. She would eventually be forgiven by her husband; she was always loved by her children; she must be explained by the author. And (this crept insidiously into my thoughts) there might even be a hint that she would reform. Because she *has* been frightened; she *is* getting older; she *has* a religious ancestry and shows traces of it in her superstitiousness.

I debated this a long time and eventually put it in—but so faint a hint that only a few noticed it.

Louise habitually improvised on the piano. Her husband was accustomed to hearing this. After their reunion, he realizes she is playing harmonies she has never played before. It makes him wonder. And so the reader can wonder. For what else could this mean but that her soul has been shaken and is emitting cries it never could have emitted before?

My house was finished in August. Reese gave me the name for it, "Tyrawley," after a far-back Irish ancestor.

But I couldn't endure the confusion and noise and crates and smells of paint and varnish. I would put Kim in the car and escape to Cape Cod.

Reese says I never stopped talking about my book and he never got tired of listening.

Louise was not the only villain—there was Ramsey, too. And I found myself very reluctant to write about him. It is as if I cannot really believe in villains. I marvel (enviously) at those writers who can make a whole interesting book about a villain.

In one of my earliest screen conferences, I paid a compliment to a director who had put such a character into a picture. "Yes," the director said complacently, "a very dirty heavy."

There was not a single heavy in any book I had ever written. Not even anyone who was mean or cruel. Now I had to do this really *very dirty heavy*—Ramsey.

I tried to dodge it. Suppose his villainy was performed before the story opens? Suppose the reader only learns of him when Louise confesses to her husband that she had once had an affair with him? Or when the question of the paternity of Joyce comes up? Or I could introduce him and show him in flashbacks only. Experimenting, I wrote a scene between Ramsey and Samuel at Marshlands when Ramsey hints that Joyce is his, not Samuel's.

In my discussion with Reese on the *Tinavire*, we had argued the possibility or even probability that some one of the children might not be Samuel's. If there were to be such a complication, it should, obviously, involve Ramsey. (Anyone else would be too far afield.) Nothing else would so strengthen and motivate the conflict between the two brothers and the violence of Samuel's revulsion against his wife. It could quite reasonably unhinge Samuel's mind and bring all sorts of cataclysms in its train.

Moreover, what else could so solidly turn Ramsey into a "very dirty heavy"? Here was exactly what I needed. And yet I disliked it and felt a revulsion against it; so trite, so hackneyed, so mid-Victorian and old-fashioned. But what nonsense! How can such a thing ever be old-fashioned any more than getting up in the morning and going to bed at night? It is all around us—as common as apples.

It would require complicated mechanics, but to a veteran screen writer this was just good sport.

... let's see ... seven- or eight-month baby ... no, why not exactly full term born just nine months after marriage ... leave the paternity forever in doubt ... the whole family gathered at Marshlands for the wedding ... only a corridor separating the particular bedrooms involved ... only the testimony of the old nurse (Maggie Donohue) as to the night wandering down that corridor which had made that nurse forever certain that Ramsey was Joyce's father. ...

I wrote all this plot out.

It was rather exciting. If it was to stand alone as the climax of a book, everything hanging on that one fact, it would be fairly good material (overlooking the matter of the triteness). But it did not stand alone; and just briefly sketched in to cover certain plot requirements, I saw that it would clutter and overweigh and interfere.

Possibly when I got close to it there might appear a way to bring it in. Besides, could I do without it? That was always the final test. At the present moment I did not see how I could.

I wrote other scenes for Ramsey, all of them flashbacks, fairly well on in the book. I wanted the ground clear in all the early chapters for the introductions of Samuel, Louise, and the children.

There was the possibility that Ramsey, too, ought to be brought in at the first, and presented in person to the reader, instead of in a flashback; but I shrank from doing this. I really had not yet mastered Ramsey and kept pushing him away. But as I wrote these flashback scenes for him, I became aware that they had no solidity at all. The trouble might be in Ramsey himself; or it might be in the way I was presenting him. I did not, at that time, know.

Eventually I had to bring him in at the very beginning, and in person. I succeeded so well with him that Kent said, "I hated Ramsey so much that when I had been reading about him I couldn't sleep at night." And when I was still doubtful, he added, "I don't see how he could have been done better."

Certain critics, too, picked out Ramsey as the best characterization of the book. I still disagree.

But meanwhile I had the other characters to work at.

I was not too disturbed about my hero. I knew there was a problem, and sooner or later it must be met and solved. It was the very size of the problem that allowed me to be calm about it, for it was the whole book. If I could not create that character, I simply could not do the book, and I would give it up.

In a way, I gave it up in advance. It was always possible I had attempted something beyond me. But I did not think I had. I would just bide my time. I did not want to do anything forced. Something should simply dawn upon me about Samuel.

The introduction of a character is of the first importance. It is not enough to show him in a truly characteristic action, the first scene must guide the reader's reaction to the exactly right feeling about him.

Once, in the movies, they made a picture about Richard Coeur de Lion, with Wally Beery playing the lead.

He was introduced devouring a leg of mutton, holding it by the bone in one hand as if it was a big chop, waving it around as he talked and shouted with great hunks of it

[99]

protruding from his mouth. The audience rocked with laughter. This was the historical figure whom we know as the Lionhearted, a hero capable of firing our youth to deeds of valor (such as the flying of the Atlantic, alone). And there was but one short bit of film that could be devoted to the introduction; and on the score of realism and period business he was shown mauling a joint like a dog in a corner.

First impressions are hard to overcome.

I had not so far succeeded in making my readers take the right attitude toward my hero. I needed some sort of a miracle. Finally I got it. So simple!

Evelyn D—— came up to see me, and I read her some of the scenes I had written. She said, "Why does he have to have the name of Samuel?" And she made a face.

Evelyn can express a world of disgust with just one small grimace. And in that instant I knew I had never liked my hero's name.

Why had I called him that? The little picture that hung over his crib in his nursery—the infant Samuel kneeling up and saying, "Speak, Lord, for thy servant heareth"—this had seemed to me a good reason for making my hero's name the same. For so it would be natural for him to identify himself with the pictured child and thus dedicate himself to the ministry.

But it was not in the least necessary. And I had constantly stumbled and tripped over the name when I wanted his wife or friend to speak to him familiarly. Would they call him Sam? And wasn't there something *soft* about Samuel? Would a boy like it for his name?

So now my hero changed from Samuel to Bartholomew.

[100]

He gained in stature. His voice went deeper. They would naturally call him Bart. Even I, the author, could, I thought, call him Bart. Ramsey, belittling him, would call him Bats or Batty. It seemed ready made. This had been his real name all along. Why hadn't I known it? Louise, in her moments of tenderness, called him Barthie. . . .

An enormous handicap was removed from the book with this change. I felt sure that the prejudice against my hero that I had noticed in the men with whom I had talked of him—Whit and Reese, Frank and Mark and Leigh—would not have existed if he had been rightly named from the start.

So, in an instant, comes progress. Just keep on . . . keep on. . . .

Sixteen

THIS IS THE summer that Reese, wanting to lop off the branch of a pine tree, climbed it with an ax in his hand and gave the branch some mighty blows. The ax slipped.

When I got to Wellfleet he was still limping, still bandaged; and he showed me the deep slash in his instep and told me of his difficulty in getting from the woods to the house because of the blood he was losing; and what the doctor had said and done.

It reminds me now as I write of it, of those Wyngate children and the things that were always happening to them at Kennebunkport. "What children!" exclaimed Deirdre when she came to read of them.

But I have to write of children as I know them. We four had certainly been such children; nearly drowned, nearly broken in falls, nearly gored by bulls, burned in fires. But only in a general sense did the Wyngates draw life from us—they drew life from another source too.

I once heard described the family of an Episcopalian clergyman who lived in the country and plowed his fields while he pondered his sermons. He had seven daughters of surpassing beauty. The talk hinged on the question, Is there anything in the legendary idea that spirituality bestows physical loveliness?

I had heard of that before. I had heard a priest expressing regret that when the little children are presented at the altar rail for their first Communion they close their eyes, open their mouths, stick out their tongues (as they have been taught), and so make hideous little monsters of themselves, whereas, being pious and spiritual children, they should be just the ones to have an ideal beauty.

I had never forgotten this. It seemed to me natural and right that, though one single lifetime of spirituality might produce only a beautiful expression, a beautiful smile, beautiful light in the eye, several generations might be expected to produce the actual physical beauty as well.

My Wyngates had been a spiritual family for generations; so they must be beautiful.

In my thirty-page exposition, I had shown Adam, the father, plowing his fields while he ruminated his sermons. I had invented the little boy, Samuel (now Bartholomew), walking in the furrow behind him, talking with him. And for use later on in the story, the seven beautiful daughters became the six beautiful children of Bartholomew and Louise.

In bringing these children to life I was really carried away by my love for them. They excited me. I could have painted each exquisite little face, even the face of Jennifer, the ugly duckling, who feared that she was a disgrace to her handsome family and always apologized as she made her little curtsy to a stranger, "I am at the ugly age."

In such a bevy of beauties, there is always one who is

the most beautiful. I sought in my memory for the most beautiful girl I had ever seen and found her in a friend of my adolescence. She had simply dazzled us all. She had abundant softly waving hair of spun gold; long almond eyes of deep blue shaded by sweeping dark lashes, vivid red cupid's bow mouth (we argued about the shade of red and the exact shape), a slim, lissome figure, and wild-rose skin. And I heard the grownups discussing her. In fact, she provided the theme for a disproportionate amount of talk that summer, which conveyed to me a sense of the importance of beauty. I thought much about it. Why has one got it and another not? What sort of destiny does it confer? The destiny, so far as I could see it then, was that males fell prostrate before her and people of both sexes kept looking at her.

That girl's later destiny was, in actuality, a tragic one. For in the year that she came out she fell deeply in love with a married man. They could not be wed. She could not forget and recover. She married someone else; had a daughter; at last lost her mind and was put away. The daughter killed herself.

I remembered a few other girls with beauty that was out of the ordinary. Not one had a life that a mother would want for her girl.

One of my Wyngates, the eldest, Joyce, should have this beauty and the tragic destiny. She, too, when she was very young must fall in love with a married man. He came to life for me instantly. I could see him, with his small romantic blond mustache. He found his right name easily, Richard Edelman, and he was the German-born assistant organist at Bartholomew's church. He gave piano lessons to the Wyngate girls. This was an entirely imaginary character, owing nothing to anyone I have ever seen.

Jennifer, the third girl, the ugly duckling, adored this older sister and became her confidante. These two girls moved through their well-ordered lives in the big Brooklyn house of the Wyngates (by the way, how did a clergyman come to have such a house? Well—inherited money and the gifts of a wealthy older sister—easily such plot details fall into place). The strict German governess kept them in order. This was our own "Frill"—dead these many years. Between Joyce and Jennifer was the other sister, Sara, proud and aloof and critical, safe in her passionate closeness to Cecil, the oldest son. The two little ones, Cherry and Runo, had their own attachment and their own life.

The confusion at Tyrawley gradually gave way to order. We moved in. Bertha came to keep house for me and discovered that a dog can be an important member of a family.

"Why, Kim is a person!" she exclaimed.

We acquired, too, a couple of tiny yellow kittens, which Kim welcomed with motherly warmth. They crawled over his shaggy coat and lay in the hollows of his thighs and forepaws.

I began to feel at home in the new-old house. It was pleasant to have Bertha in charge of it, to hear her voice at my door every morning, "Good morning, Miss O'Hara," and then see her come in carrying my breakfast tray followed by Kim, grinning, head down, wagging his tail.

I wrote so much that, before long, my papers almost swamped me. They were all over my room in piles, corners, put away in drawers, on shelves.

From time to time one reads of writers inventing their own work tables. One, I remember, had a rounded tier of steps like a small amphitheater at one end of the room. The writer sat before his table with his back to these steps. His papers were put into divisions in the risers, so that he could whirl around in his chair and all those pigeonholes would face him.

Another writer worked at a long horseshoe shaped table in a horseshoe shaped room under a high glass dome. Set into the floor, close to the table, was a slotted steel rail. Her chair had a peg that fitted into this slot, so that she could slide around the table without rising. (I have wondered what virtue there is in that? It rests me to be made to rise frequently, walk, bend, stretch, and reach.)

Dreiser had a long room with shelves that ran the length of the wall, and his papers were piled upon them.

I have found that a small room, a mere nook, is better to think in. Your thoughts don't escape into outer space. So I converted a small dressing room off my bedroom to this use and designed myself a desk.

Erik Olsen, the Swedish foreman-carpenter who had built my house, made it for me.

First, a flat strong table four and a half by three feet. (I found this—a beautiful antique pine table.) Then, at the back, Erik built a double tier of pigeonholes, each the size of a box of typewriting paper, eight in all. These are for paper, carbons, finished chapters, discards, etc., and form a little bench. From this rises a two-and-a-half-foot bookcase, partitioned vertically into three panels. Each panel holds six shelves of thin plywood tipped so they slant sharply down backwards, more vertical than horizontal. This forms eighteen tilted slots, each a little larger than the usual folder. These slots are for folders, each folder labeled with the names of characters or places or events or chapters, depending on how I wish to classify my material. The flap of every folder with its label is directly in front of my eyes and within reach of my hand. The typewriter sits on the table directly before me.

When I acquired this table and classified and filed all my notes, an enormous load of confusion was lifted from me. No disorder was possible. The smallest scrap of a note could not elude me for long. And my eyes, scanning the labels, could in an instant take in the whole work. I had it in command.

In the right-hand panel, the six slots held six folders labeled, Joyce and Organist. Jennifer and Cadet. Scenes at Church. Children at Marshlands. Jennifer's Confession. Piano Lessons.

These folders were already crammed, and still growing.

It began to worry me that I could not stop writing about those children. There was more about the children than anything else.

Seventeen

WRITING A BOOK is all the solving of problems. I expected that. But they need not all be solved at once. Push them away and take them one at a time.

I had been pushing away the problem of Marshlands for a long time.

Not to have Marshlands in the book, not to show the children there, not to show all the characters in that easy, informal, comfortable New England setting, the summer vacation life that I know so well and like so much, was unthinkable.

I longed to do some Marshlands pages that would deliver to the reader the hot smells of the summer fields, the blackberry stains around the soft little mouths, the excited barkings of the dogs, the sound of the surf on the shore, and the emotions of the children in this setting. The ecstasy. If I could just deliver one impact of that—really do it to my own satisfaction . . .

A story can be told about; or told. The difference is like the difference between deliberate remembering and actually re-experiencing a moment out of a distant past, as when there comes a faraway sound, or a whiff of fragrance; and one stands stunned—*How that takes me back!*

This is pure sensation. This was what I wanted to achieve. Hardly a day that my thoughts did not reach out to this hope and softly circle around it; for it cannot be forced. Hardly a day that I did not, on the typewriter, improvise a little scene: Cherry in the spring house while Mrs. Gooch churns; Runo on the ridgepole of the roof; Jennifer in the crow's nest; all of them together trooping up the stream. Then, without any critical appraisal of what I had done, I would file the scene away. The folder labeled Summer at Marshlands was getting very thick.

But the real problem was this. Though I would probably succeed in writing it as I wished, I did not see how I could ever get it into the book. For in the beginning I must create the Brooklyn atmosphere. It is not done in a few sentences. It takes chapters. And to my way of thinking there is no more irritating construction than to leave a well-established, well-liked background in the middle of a book, go away, and begin to build another somewhere else.

Your reader has to go along with you, as a dancing partner goes along in a dance. Sometimes a dancing partner gets balky, and there's an argument between feet. The old rule, *Observe the unities,* has been broken. You shatter the unity of place by going off to parts unknown. It is a shock to your dancing partner, and he will follow you now reluctantly, dragging his weight.

But how could I avoid this? Obviously, I had to begin in Brooklyn and then go to Marshlands, or begin in Marshlands and then go to Brooklyn.

There are devices—I could begin in Brooklyn and bring in all the Marshlands parts in flashbacks; or vice versa. Begin by making a careful division of the story material, deciding which parts to place in the country, which in the city.

I saw no other way, but it did not please me. Retrospects have to be different in pace and style. They are apt to be difficult reading. It is hard for the reader to get so completely into a retrospect that he really forgets the other and can settle down to a leisurely, continuous flow. And if you do succeed in making him do this, then you shock him again when you force him to go back to the original time and place. There was no hope, if I did it this way, that I would ever be able to deliver those vignettes of childhood ecstasies in the country. That's the kind of thing you cannot, with truth, put into a retrospect. If you do, some editor is going to want it out.

I hoped that when I actually set myself at this task I would get an inspiration. I hoped for a miracle.

Meanwhile I was receiving from time to time letters from Lippincott, inquiring as to the progress of the book; asking if I could name a date?

And October was passing. And though we were in the middle of Indian Summer I knew the weather might change any day.

Sooner or later I must pay a visit to Kennebunkport. I had never actually been there. I woke up to the fact with startled suddenness.

I knew a good deal about it. It had been the summer home of my first husband, Kent's father, and he had talked of his childhood there. Moreover, I knew similar places from summer visits during my childhood; I knew the East Coast, the Atlantic seaboard resorts; I knew the New England atmosphere, for my forebears had come from New England. I knew it, too, from much reading.

But this was not enough. Just exactly what was the line of the Kennebunkport coast? What beaches? Cliffs? Caves? Rocky points? What depth to the harbor? How many masts to the ships that came in there? What industries? What kind of soil? Trees? Flowers? Could you see the mountains north and inland? Could you see Mount Katahdin? Where did the river flow? How deep? Shipping in it or not? What fishing? And a host of other such questions. I wrote them down. Long lists.

I could not write the Marshlands summer scenes until I had firsthand knowledge of all this.

Fiction writers do not have to be faithful to facts if they do not wish to be. Houses can be moved here or there. Shore lines changed. Points of scenic interest invented. But when I am departing from fact I like to know how wide my departure is.

I must go to Kennebunkport right away. Why, the winter snows might be upon us, country roads impassable—and the book must be finished before the spring!

I telephoned Reese in New York, but he was tied up with a case and could not accompany me. It was the same with my sisters and a couple of friends; Kim and I took off alone.

It was a weather breeder of a day; and what I met when I got there was one of the typical equinoctial storms of the North Shore, a truly awe-inspiring sight.

I had brought with me only light summer things, ginghams and barefoot sandals, thinking the heat would hold, and it is worse to be too warmly dressed than too thinly. You can always get warm (so I thought!).

The way I got warm on that visit, warm enough to keep life in me, was to take about three long hot baths a day. The one hotel that was open had no furnace but did have hot water. I envied Kim his thick fur coat.

I stayed three days, found the site for Marshlands, saw plenty of woods, trees, flowers, beaches, the lagoon; filled a notebook with questions and answers and finally came upon a treasure-trove in a booklet containing the history of the town. I had a long talk with a "native." Yes—on a clear day, you could see Mount Katahdin from that little hill there.

The only coat I had with me was a thin so-called waterproof. It was no proof against that storm. I would go out and walk around for an hour or so; then, wet through and with chattering teeth, hurry back to the hotel for another hot bath.

Again and again I returned to the beach to stand watching the combers roll in, rise, explode, and hurl themselves on the shore.

When I left, stopping at every roadside mailbox to note the local names, my little book was full.

I met much traffic coming the other way. Half the state, it seemed, wanted to see the storm and the wrecks on the shore. At places, hundreds of cars were halted or slowly milling; traffic officers at every intersection.

There would be storms, I thought, in my book. You couldn't live on the North Shore and not know about storms. They got into your blood.

This visit supplied me with all the necessary background material. And yet it did not solve the basic problem.

I now built the house to which I gave the name of Marshlands, put it there near the town, near the sea, near the lagoon; and put into it the sleeping family with their dreams and fears and hopes and the touch of wind and dawn and sunrise. The house bore a decided resemblance to my grandmother's house at Deercreek, where I had spent most of the summers of my childhood.

The writing went well now; that is, fluently. The children at Kennebunkport; Cecil saving a summer visitor from drowning; Cecil thrown and dragged by the horse; Runo setting the house on fire. (It was Kent who had done that at Santa Cruz when he was five, and the Mayor came riding on the fire engine and said, "What kind of kids has this woman got anyway?")

It may be wondered why I went on and on with all this writing about the children when, deep down within me, I knew perfectly well it could never all go into the book. The answer was, firstly, I simply could not bear to stop it. And secondly, I knew it was good stuff. According to my principle of keeping the windows open and letting anything fly in that wanted to, I would keep on until the flow stopped—and someday, perhaps, I might use some of the scenes in something else.

But there came a day when I stopped writing and put the cover on my typewriter and said to myself, Either you throw out nine-tenths of what you have written about the children and get on with your proper story, or you must make two books of it. One of them will be called *The Wyngate Children.*

There had actually come about one of those conflagrations of which Kent and I had talked in Paris; out there behind me was a complete story. *Locale,* Brooklyn and Marshlands. *Body of thought,* my knowledge of children. *Subject,* the Wyngate children. *Theme,* ugly duckling. *Point of view,* omniscient author. *Protagonist,* Jennifer.

I now gave all my thought to this book, inspecting it from every angle. Why would it not be a better book for me to follow up the Flicka books with—more acceptable to my readers—than the clergyman book? It would be a quiet, family book, showing the children at home; their daily lives; the characters unfolding one by one. Not dramatic—a family book.

I got *Little Women* out of the library and reread it. I was charmed. I thought it was as good today as it ever had been. I spoke of it to people. Everyone smiled remembering it. Everybody likes and rereads that book.

I realized I had more than an abstract of *The Wyngate Children* book; I had the plot. Jennifer falls in love with Pinky, the West Point cadet, who is in love with Joyce, who is in love with the organist. Many of the scenes were written. Actually, this book was more advanced than *The Son of Adam Wyngate.* And I could write that one later.

Two books instead of one! It dawned on me like a delightful Christmas surprise.

Eighteen

THERE WERE several snags in this plan that I did not discover until much later. The first was that casual idea—not a dramatic book but a family book.

This was a break for freedom on my part, for I knew I was a dramatic writer, not only by nature but by training. But did that have to put shackles on me? Was I never to be allowed to wander comfortably along as many another writer does?

But one's nature does put shackles on one. And training too.

It is only in these latter years that I have come to realize that when I was in Hollywood I had an exceptional opportunity to learn from a veritable fountainhead of knowledge.

George Pierce Baker, Professor of Dramatics, first at Harvard and then at Yale, was at that time conducting the famous class that had come to be called Workshop 47. From his tutelage in playwrighting, dramatic construction, and play doctoring or "carpentering" have come a succession of famous playwrights: Eugene O'Neill, Winchell Smith, Joshua Logan, Philip Barry, *et al.*

One of these playwrights, Winchell Smith, after some Broadway successes, went to Hollywood to put one of his plays on the screen; and there I met him and, for the first time in my life, heard the name of George Pierce Baker. (This was many years before I wrote *My Friend Flicka.*)

Winchell Smith stayed in Hollywood a year, learning screen technique. He found his best teacher, assistant, and collaborator in one of the young editors at the studio, a man of unusual dramatic talent. Arthur Ripley, who has since become a director and producer, was then the head of the cutting department, and I was working with him. He taught Winchell Smith the screen; Winchell Smith taught him George Pierce Baker. And I, thus, by a sort of apostolic succession, received instruction that was an echo of an echo of an echo of what George Pierce Baker was at that time teaching in Workshop 47 at Yale.

So it happened that I had received thorough schooling in dramatic writing, and when I wrote *My Friend Flicka,* the book bore the stamp of it.

The New York critics and editors could not figure it out. A magazine editor who was considering buying it asked, "Is it really on the level? She didn't steal it? Because no one ever heard of her before."

After the book's initial success, Lippincott gave a luncheon for me. They asked twenty top critics. Twenty accepted and came.

Lewis Gannett of the *New York Herald Tribune,* seated beside me, was insistent with his questions. "Is it really your first novel? Haven't you a lot of others—unfinished perhaps—piled up on the shelf in a closet?"

But there really were not; and so I told him.

"But first novels are not like this," he insisted. "Where did you learn to write, then?"

"In the movies."

This puzzled him still further. Authors, he said, did not learn how to write in the movies; they learned how not to write.

I finally began to feel puzzled myself. I did not know enough to say, "Well, in a way—a very long-distance way—it might be said that I learned to write in Workshop 47."

There may be some truth in it, but when you learn from a disciple (and who is not one?) you don't know quite how much you are learning from the disciple and how much from the disciple's master. I learned from Arthur Ripley, who was to some degree a disciple of Winchell Smith, who was a disciple of George Pierce Baker.

Winchell Smith and I had some talks together before he left the studio, mostly about Ripley.

He said, "You know, whenever I have finished a scene, I have to wait for Rip to tell me, good, bad, or indifferent. And what he says *goes*."

I felt the same.

I was a novice at screen work. Ripley taught me how to put a picture together after it had been "shot"—a reverse action for me; for a scenarist writes, before the picture is made, the scenes that are then photographed by the cameraman under the orders of the director. The separate shots are glued together in the cutting room according to the scene numbers on the original script

[117]

(for quite likely they have not been shot in chronological sequence). Now you have the finished picture. If it is unsatisfactory, or too long, it is "doctored"; taken to pieces. The hundreds of separate shots are rolled up individually and filed, to be reassembled in different order or length. Possibly extra shots may be needed to fill in some hiatus, and this is done if the actors can be called back. (Of course, their work was over when the camera stopped grinding and they have long since left the studio.) This was before the talkies, and the "spoken title" or "narrative title" told a great deal of the story. These "titles" are the words and sentences that appear right on the screen. By changing them and writing new ones, you can change the effect of the picture to an astonishing degree.

Such play doctoring takes great skill, and Ripley was expert at it. He had salvaged numbers of pictures that would otherwise never have been released. On a job of this sort he needed a writer from the scenario department to collaborate with him and write the titles, and he picked me.

I cannot imagine better training for a future dramatist or dramatic writer. I held those scenes—just strips of celluloid—in my hands. I put them first in one order, then another. The necessity of keeping yourself to a certain length was something not to be argued with, you had just so many feet to do it in. Now and then, when thousands of feet of film had to be taken out yet somehow the story kept intact and clearly told, I would have to write a narrative title that would be a marvel of condensation. There were boys in the department who glued the strips together in whatever order we wished to try them. (I still use scissors and scotch tape and pins, snipping my pages to bits, gluing paragraphs together again in different order.)

There was, for our exclusive use, a small projection room with screen and projector. We could get the finished effect of as many different arrangements of material in a sequence as we wished. Ripley and I tried them exhaustively.

With this training behind me I became pretty good at play doctoring myself.

Later, when I had become a free-lance writer, I was called to a studio to see what I could do with a very "sick" picture.

The director had failed to show, somewhere in the middle, that the heroine had yielded to the blandishments of the villain and was no longer a virgin. As the whole denouement hinged on this, the picture didn't make sense. The director was fired, the picture put on the shelf; and there it would stay unless it could be salvaged. To introduce (by means of calling the cast back and shooting new scenes) a middle sequence that would explain what had happened didn't seem feasible. In what scenes could you show it? And nothing that anyone had thought of matched what had gone before and what followed.

I suggested doing it with a single narrative title. But they didn't think that could be done either. How could such a thing be flatly stated in a title?

This was one of those things that seem impossible until you see the way. When you do, nothing could be easier.

I wrote the title in a minute or two, and there was

nothing shocking about it. The picture was finished, released, and shown.

My hairdresser saw it—saw my name on the screen as title writer, and said to me while she was shampooing my head, "Say—she went the limit with that fellow, didn't she?"

"What made you think so?" I asked from out of the soapsuds.

"You know—where it said she had given her happiness into his keeping. . . ."

In a previous chapter I have mentioned rhythm in connection with dramatic construction; and pace; the difference between preparatory writing and climactic and winding up; and the first knowledge I had about this subject came to me from Ripley.

Here is where I learned how terrible is the effect of a flat monotone in writing. In life the pace varies from minute to minute. Fall into a brown study and an hour passes in what seems like five minutes. But just get strung up into intense anticipation and every second is an hour. You can become aware of a major catastrophe with all its ramifications while you are removing your hat.

Behind every outer act and word is an inner dynamic tension. It is like a wind blowing through the moments, blowing through *time*. And the force of that wind, varying as it does every instant, causes variations of pace in the outer physical movements. And this makes rhythm. Life is rhythmic.

Writing, then, to be lifelike, must be rhythmic, too.

If human behavior is presented in a flat monotone, you have taken out the wind; you have taken out the changes of tension, *ergo* the rhythm. Thus it is made unlifelike, indeed a travesty of life, totally unconvincing. The characters become mechanical puppets. Such writing is close to unreadable. Fortunately many writers, perhaps all "born" writers, know about this intuitively.

Many years of thinking and reading and experimenting have clarified this point for me. But I have not met many people, even literary people, who seem to have given it much thought. Most books on writing, even by the best authors, do not mention it.

I believe Whit Burnett is very conscious of it. As I said, talented people know it unconsciously. He was certainly referring to this when, once in the classroom, he made a remark about a short story I had turned in.

As it was a complimentary remark, I should here say something apologetic about the way I preen myself. This is the very difficulty I considered when I weighed the advantages and disadvantages of an I-book. If you tell of your successes you will appear conceited; but if you don't, then there will be an omission of something important, or a dull understatement, just when a child would scream, *I won!* And this will be an annoyance and frustration to the reader, for he has identified himself with you, and your triumphs are his; when you boast and put the feather in your cap he exults. In fact, it's the point of the whole book. So, as my loyalty is always to the reader, I shall omit all conventional self-deprecation.

I remember a brief apologetic for boastfulness in a book by Booth Tarkington.

On an ocean liner a number of American tycoons were assembled in the smoker, and they were boasting of their exploits. One, born a pauper, told the staggering figure of the fortune he had made; another, how in a matter of days he had turned a deal that had netted him millions; another, how by a series of bold strokes he had seized a kingdom from a competitor.

Tarkington said it was thrilling talk, an evening's conversation that would be remembered by all who were lucky enough to hear it; and he compared it to the Arab custom which demands that when the chieftains assemble for a meeting of the tribes, each one, before he can be received, must announce his possessions, his conquests, and his triumphs.

Actually, if the things I attempted in the making of my novel had not succeeded, there would be little sense in my writing this record. And when compliments were paid me, and I followed them up to ask why (as if greedy for more), I shall report it all here, for it is even more important to know what an author does admirably than what he does badly.

The case in point occurred when Whit was reading my story to the class and he suddenly stopped reading, looked up and slowly around. "Everybody in the room know who wrote this?"

There was no answer. He studied their faces a few moments longer, remarked laconically, "Only one writer in the class who could have written this—" and then went on reading.

After the class I went to him privately and asked how he knew I was the author. (The stories were never signed.)

He answered, "You're the only writer here who has the emotional drive."

He used to talk, too, about the "fictional drive," pointing out that records of adventures or harrowing lives, newspaper reports, or the experiences of war refugees did not make "stories" unless and until they were fictionized. They had no fictional drive.

The first time I was made to think about these drives (to which I now have given the name wind) was in my Hollywood office, when I had asked Ripley to read over a sequence I had written and tell me what he thought of it.

His opinions were usually slow in coming, for he was not articulate.

When he had finished it and put the pages down, he stretched out his long legs (he was a veritable jack-in-the-box) and put the tips of his long thin fingers together and bowed his head over them and fell into profound meditation. He finally said, in a quiet and conversational tone, "It's really awfully bad."

There can be only one consolation in receiving a blow of this kind. If you keep your head, you are likely to learn something. There's always a thrill in learning. I did keep my head—but I was terribly angry, angry that he had kept me in suspense, waiting and hoping for several long long minutes, when he must have known instantly what his verdict would be.

I kept silent, hoping that he would elucidate. And presently he did—a little. "I wouldn't know what to do with that when I got it in the cutting room. It's so closely knit you could hardly change it."

I had worked hard over that sequence. It was a climax;

and I had thought up a lot of effective action, swift and violent doings, and made them follow each other in rapid succession; and actually it was all in one tempo—a monotone—and I began to get glimpses of this as I talked to Rip.

Suddenly the utter artificiality of it struck me like a blow. And the silliness; and dreariness.

There was a long silence. I was in despair. All that work for nothing—I felt as if I had exhausted my inventiveness. "What on earth will I make the characters do, then?"

Out of another long meditation on his finger tips Ripley at length said, in the calm, conversational tone, "Well, let's see now—*what would they naturally do?*"

When I had finally accomplished that sequence to Ripley's satisfaction, moving the characters through their parts "as they naturally would do," they had become real and lifelike and believable. There was that *wind* blowing through the action, so that the tension seized you and then let go. It was rhythmic.

Since then I have seen many books written as I at first wrote that sequence, all in one tempo; whole books conceived, written, and published—tiresome and nearly unreadable, though with good material, plot, and characters —because they lack that one thing, that wind—the breath of life.

When I left Hollywood to embark on the Wyoming chapter of my life, I lost track of Arthur Ripley, but have heard of him from time to time since.

I last saw his name in the book *Editor to Author,* the book About Maxwell Perkins and Thomas Wolfe. On page 249 Arthur Ripley of Monter-Ripley Productions is mentioned favorably as a possible producer of Wolfe's *Look Homeward, Angel*. One of the other Scribner editors said to Perkins, "If you can get the producer of *Voice in the Wind* [Ripley] you need fear nothing."

Nineteen

For me to undertake the writing of a family book was, therefore, a considerable departure from my training as a dramatic writer. But I had no doubt of my ability to do it.

All of the editors at Lippincott were pleased, with the exception of Mark, who growled that it was disappointing to give up the "thunderous problem" of the adult characters and fill the book, instead, with a "lot of kids cutting up."

Leigh said, "A family book—I like the idea. When they are well done, they are always successful."

Whit said, "Why not three books? Probably you have generated enough energy for three. Look what you did with Flicka."

I knew that I must now very carefully divide all my material. The whole Wyngate family would of course be introduced in the first book, but any hint of the breach between the parents, which was to be the substance of the second book, must be held back.

I began *The Wyngate Children* on January 1, 1950.

Beginning a book, any book, the first thing to do is break down the whole story into parts small enough to be handled as units.

This particular book divided itself into two parts; each part into four sections; and each section into several subdivisions, to which, in a talk I once gave at Columbia University, I gave the name of "chunks."

That was the only lecture I have ever given. Lecturing is supposed to be a novelist's side line. I could never see why. If you have the ability to sit in a little room by yourself and dream up stories, why should you then be expected to possess those qualifications that would enable you to stand on platforms with a certain assurance and style, and meet hundreds or thousands of eyes and talk for an hour or two? And if you did enjoy this, and acceded to the scores of requests that are sent from the lecture agencies, would you not then have to give up your writing?

Kent refers to this single lecture I gave as "that time you were framed," and in a way, I was.

The fanfare that is the result of a first novel by an unknown author was a surprise to me, much of it quite thrilling, some of it painfully embarrassing.

But I was grateful; felt I was in the hands of my publishers who had soon become my friends, and that I must do everything they wanted me to do to help along the sales of the book. So I kept the appointments they made for me; was photographed; gave interviews; attended luncheons and cocktail parties; talked about myself;

smiled; explained my methods; wrote autobiographical sketches.

I drew the line at lecturing, either on the radio or the lecture platform. It took too much out of me. Besides, I have always suffered from stage fright if I have to open my mouth in public. (See Cherry in *The Son of Adam Wyngate*.)

They agreed to that; agreed to everything I wanted; quite spoiled me. But, indirectly, there came from Columbia University the suggestion that I might be willing to meet and talk to young people who had ambitions to become writers—I wouldn't mind doing that, would I? I said, No—not at all.

And would I be the guest of honor at a dinner given for me by the English Department of Columbia beforehand? Remember—this story had first been turned in at Columbia, so in a way, Columbia was my Alma Mater. I wouldn't mind that, would I? Oh, no—I didn't mind dinners. There's only one person on each side of you to talk to.

So there was the dinner in one of the Columbia reception rooms. I was astonished at the length of the narrow refectory table; and the plumes and aigrettes on the hats of the wives of the faculty members.

After dinner they said, "But it's not here you are going to talk to the students, it's in another room." And we trooped through some buildings and across a courtyard, and in a few moments I was entering a sort of theater or auditorium with Whit holding me firmly by one arm, and the Ph.D. who was the head of the Literary Department by the other.

There was a dais with a few large chairs like thrones in a row, and I was led to the center one. I took my seat facing the audience of students. All those pairs of eyes riveted themselves upon me.

It was simply shattering.

There was no escape.

Actually there *was* an escape—or so they have told me since. Escape of a sort. They had planned that if I closed my mouth and would not open it, they would do all the talking themselves. They would let me just sit there, and would explain and exhibit me.

But I did not know this at the time. I felt my back was to the wall. I saw I was going to have to talk; I was going to have to answer the urgent questions in all those student eyes; I was going to have to give a lecture and a good one.

That I was completely unprepared was my salvation. I had to forget myself, my voice, my stage fright, my nervousness, and think about my subject. I had a few minutes to do it in. Fortunately, I usually do my best when my back is to the wall.

Whit stood up and introduced me in a leisurely fashion. Then the Doctor of Philosophy took the floor and walked up and down it, slowly and easily (what *sang-froid!*), explaining that I had done something that had never been done at Columbia before. He named the millions of copies of my first book that had been printed and then the millions of copies of the sequel. . . .

Though I heard him, as he went on and on, I was concentrating on what I had to do. What, I asked myself, is the very first question a would-be author has to decide? Obviously, what to write about. So I would talk about the choice of a subject.

I had noticed in Whit's class that the students chose the strangest subjects, like the French writers who write about America gangsters, or ape Hemingway. Many of them obviously slanted their stuff at the sophisticated magazines and avoided just those subjects which it would be natural, and therefore easy, for them to write about.

I would tell them to write about the thing they loved. Was there some subject they were so interested in they made themselves a nuisance talking about it? Write about that.

I was soon talking, expatiating upon this. They asked questions and led me on. It went very easily.

I had another point in mind—the difficulty of dealing with the whole subject at once. It is as if, in the case of the inexperienced writer, he takes one deep breath and tries to rush through the book to the end; whereas the practical thing to do is to divide it into units that can be dealt with separately.

Many books are divided into parts. And all of them into chapters. But there are other, smaller divisions that can be made. Write it in chunks. Every writer has a pace of his own. My own pace led me to write chapters approximating ten pages in length; and there were about six of these in one chunk.

I talked a long time; it got slightly uproarious, and the auditorium was full of a sort of tingling electric tension.

At the end I wanted to know if anything I had said

would be at all helpful, and a number of them shouted, "Write it in chunks!"

The advice is as good for me as it was for them.

I had now to deal with the first chunk of *The Wyngate Children*.

Twenty

KENT HAS asked me to be very specific about the exact steps I take as the story moves from my mind to paper. "Do you plan a week's work in advance and then go by that plan?"

"No. There never seems to be time to figure out a plan like that. And how could I know what I would want to be doing each day?"

"How do you know what to do then, the first thing in the morning when you go to your desk?"

"I go on with one of the thousand things I didn't get done yesterday."

"Little things or big things?"

"Whichever I feel like doing. It's all got to be done sooner or later."

Whichever I feel like doing. That was it. You feel differently one day from another, and every hour of the day. And there are all kinds of work, and many different faculties to use.

The different faculties divide themselves in the main

into two classifications, which I call *hot* (the creative) and *cold* (the critical).

I have both of these faculties, and I used to think as a matter of course that all writers had them. But I have discovered that many do not.

Mark Haverford once said to me, "With a lot of writers, the more they work over their manuscript the worse it gets. But with you it keeps getting better. And you never stop. You ship the manuscript to us from California. Before it arrives comes a telegram saying pages such and such are to be changed, or a whole new opening. Before we've fairly read it, you arrive by plane, take it away from us, and change it some more. And after it's printed, you have the plates changed at your own expense."

Sometimes the hot mind and the cold mind work together in the most delightful collaboration, a friendly argument. As soon as the hot mind has put something on paper, the cold mind is pointing out how it can be improved or why it cannot be there at all.

But for the most part they do their work separately, even on separate days. Each wants the whole stage to itself. And the author should pay attention and give them their way.

On some days, the author is immediately aware that the hot mind is ready to go. The imagination takes over. Thought is poured onto paper—one, two, three, five, or ten pages at the rate of about one page every four minutes (double-spaced typing). It is exactly as if a dancer suddenly rises, bows, says, Now I will dance—and off she floats; wild and free and yet beautifully precise and controlled.

In my own case this inspirational writing (which I call "free writing") cannot be commanded. Something touches it off, and there is the dancer floating away. It is a glorious pleasure and yet it leaves one drained. You don't know that until you get up from the typewriter when it is over and find yourself unsteady. It is so important that whenever it can be done it should be done. Drop everything to get it on paper. It may be you will never use it. Possibly your imagination has taken fire from something that is slightly off the story line; but often these inspirational outpourings stand in the finished book as first written, and to excellent advantage.

I could never do this free writing if my head were aching. I don't think I could do it if I were expecting an important visitor, or even telephone call. The dancer would simply not leave her seat.

The functions of the cold mind are, of course, breaking down, analyzing, weighing, comparing, eliminating, planning, judging, delivering final verdicts—and these all in different degrees, from the crossing out of a word or a comma up to that final testing, which I call "scanning," which is so terrible a mental strain that I put off doing it as long as I can. When it must be done, it leaves me in a state resembling shock for several days. I cannot see anyone. Can hardly speak. Scanning is not the same as rereading. Simple rereading has to be done all the time. Almost as soon as anything is written it is reread and corrected as a matter of course.

But scanning is the effort to grasp whichever unit I am

examining, as a whole; to swallow it with one great gulp and know the taste and flavor in its fullness and in all its parts. To achieve this the attention must be held in absolute unwavering concentration and one-pointedness while the whole section is read, perhaps several hundred pages. I usually do it on my feet in the middle of the room, and do it so fast that my hand is in almost constant, slow, even motion, turning the pages. I could not scan a whole book at one time; but I did more than once scan half.

But this faculty is not mine to command either. My critical sense is functioning, or it is not. I have sometimes gone to New York to shop. I have even tried on the clothes, only to discover that I cannot judge in the least. It is as if I cannot see. Or, dressing in my room, I find that I have no faculty that will tell me which scarf to put on. As fast as I try one I take it off and try another. I cannot find a place to stop.

I never try to appraise my work if my critical faculty is not functioning. I do some of the drudgery instead. The greater part of all work is drudgery; the novelist must know that before he starts.

But if, early in the day, I become aware of that inner searchlight turning this way and that, illuminating dark places, clearing up confusion, delivering unanswerable verdicts, I feel a leap of exultation. I lay other work aside. I seize some part I have been wanting to scan, waiting to scan, take the manuscript into my hands, and go into the middle of the room. If I can stay on my feet long enough, keep my eyes open and seeing long enough, and my brain on the alert, I can then pass a judgment upon my work that is, within the limits of my capacity, practically infallible.

To my delight I have found that I can praise myself as well as blame. The praise is usually vocal. "This is really good." "Why, Mary! A marvelous scene!" And once I heard myself say in slow, wondering tones (I had scanned a couple of hundred pages that I had not looked at for months), "This—is—so—good—I—am—astounded!"

But when I am displeased, which is far more often, I am grimly silent. I sink into—not despair, which would still have some life and feeling, but weariness and indifference. My mental faculties fade until I feel only partially conscious.

It is experience that has taught me, when I begin work in the mornings, to examine myself and discover which of my faculties is in the ascendant.

What causes this fluctuation I do not know. Perhaps half-realized preoccupations; perhaps dreams; perhaps the weather. I never combat it.

Twenty-one

THE WYNGATE CHILDREN was to be written in continuity (since I had the plot) beginning at page one, chapter one.

In selecting that amount of story which would form the first chunk, I listened for the *wind*. Rhythm must dictate the length of it, not the number of pages or the plot steps. There is a curve. The tension begins, tightens a little, at last relaxes a little—pauses. There is the end of the first chunk. This is a subtle thing and a variable too; for the the way one writes it can increase or decrease the tension. One does not always find that correct pause at the first effort.

Having chosen the chunk, I estimated the number of chapters it would contain. This, too, is a guess. I thought, in this case, it would be eight.

I chose eight folders. I wrote an outline of the plot each chapter would contain, and clipped this on the front of the folder. I titled each chapter for ease in memorizing them. I then went through all my notes (what a job!) and slipped into each folder whatever material was pertinent to that section of plot.

Whenever I am doing this sort of work, which I call "blocking out," new ideas come, and I catch them and type them off and put them into their proper folders. If a big scene comes in its entirety, I drop all other work, write it, and put it in its place.

When all this has been done, I must allow considerable time, some days probably, before beginning to write. For this is merely the framework; and the subconscious mind must get on the job of filling it in. Also, the critical mind must weigh the bits and acts and scenes and episodes, handling each one to make sure that it is logical, has sufficient weight, is not only credible but true. Judging it also as to economy. Can it be dispensed with? Simplified? Just how are the plot steps to be disclosed so that there shall be no glimpse of the wheels going around?

And lastly, and most important and difficult of all, I must discover which of these bits of action (the plot steps) will finally disclose itself as the climax, and thus show me which part of the action has to be written in preparatory tempo, which climactic, and which winding up.

There has to be a choice made between the different plot steps. A peculiar choice, as if one bit of action were superior to another.

. . . there is a hierarchy of events . . . some have greater rank and weight than others . . . those of the first rank must be treated differently from those of lesser rank. . . . Also rank is not absolute but relative. . . . A certain event on a certain day means nothing . . . let it occur in different circumstances and it is stupendous. . . . I have to find the real climax before I can arrange all this preparatory material according to its proper rank and I haven't found it yet. . . . It's now about twelve . . .

[138]

I've been working since four . . . have made considerable progress but this is really a tough problem. . . .

. . . must *must* be definite about the climax in this first section. . . . There seem to be three possibilities, three plot steps of equal importance . . . but they are not really equal . . . there's no such thing as equality . . . analyze and weigh until I find the exact hierarchy . . . drop the three in a bucket of water, then watch . . . watch. . . . At first they seem to float at equal depths . . . gradually one proves to have more weight . . . sinks more rapidly . . . will ground itself first. . . . Strange business . . . how can there, as it were, be class distinctions in events? . . . But there are . . . there will be class distinctions in everything —events, places, people, schools, neighborhoods, houses, manners, literally everything—as long as we have those words in the English language—good, better, best. . . . One hears of the best people . . . now pick the best plot step. . . .

. . . remember, too, the hierarchy in methods of presentation . . . the *best* presentation for the *best* scene—not the flashback or a recollection or a letter—all these are indirect presentations and less good—but direct . . . right in the present moment . . . eye to eye . . . the exactly painted scene. . . . This is the *best* . . . save it for the *best* material. . . . Hard to discover at this stage for everything vibrates so . . . go on, go on, feel your way . . . suddenly some small things, a fan waving or a half-heard exclamation, become the key to everything, the most important of them all and you have your climax. . . .

Quite early in my work on a certain chunk I discover that there are points about which I am uncertain. This is of the greatest importance, for until these obscurities are cleared up, I cannot proceed. (Sometimes published books have obscurities in them, which readers are quick to discover.)

I locate these points of uncertainty, write them in the form of questions, and pin them on the bulletin board of my desk, which is right in front of my face. (There are, actually, three bulletin boards, each one being the lowest of the tilted shelves that hold the folders. They are made of soft wood, so that my thumbtacks can penetrate them easily.)

When those questions have struck my eyes a sufficient number of times, they begin to answer themselves. I then rewrite them in the form of short statements and pin them up again. They are now plot steps, and, usually, important ones. Such a one is likely to discover itself, in the end, a climax.

Put it together, reread; change; put together differently; reread; change again. Over and over. Here is where I use scissors, pins, and glue.

Russ Mason asked me one day, "How's the book coming along, Mary?"

"Not coming along at all, Russ. I'm stuck."

"Do tell!"

"I've run out of pins."

He bought a paper of pins and presented them to me. By mutual agreement he became Permanent Purveyor of Pins.

Often I think of bits to put in, ten or twenty at once, each belonging in a different part. This frightens and confuses me, for I can't write them all at once, my panic makes fugitives of them, and each one seems a priceless, never-to-be-found-again jewel of thought. With a pencil I put down single words rapidly, key words, hoping to anchor the whole idea. Sometimes it does. I type those I can remember on separate slips of paper and pin each one to the page where it can be inserted. I really might call this the "barrage of the bits." It is very painful, and I never get over it.

I do not let myself forget the constant, ever present danger that with all my care in organizing and reorganizing, these sentences I am writing, these paragraphs and pages (each of which represents a certain amount of force) could be so arranged that they would negate each other. And the end result would be a static book.

I've talked with Kent about the "force diagrams" that engineers use to illustrate the forces acting on an airplane. Small arrows and lines designate the lift and weight; thrust and drag; all are there on the paper; and the end result of this stupendous amount of force *could be nothing at all*. "You could build it," he said almost gleefully, "so that it couldn't move."

So also could you build a chapter; or a section; or a book.

Gradually through this endless organization and re-organization, which I call "juggling," the outline of the climax of this first chunk begins to appear. Two or three plot steps, which at first scrutiny seemed one as good as the other, begin to show a difference in importance. They grade themselves. Protocol is observed. The climax takes shape. Other material that logically leads up to it is put in order. Those scenes that cannot enhance it in any way are cut out or pared to nothing.

Every day my wastebasket goes out full to overflowing.

There was at that time an anecdote in the *Reader's Digest* that alarmed Bertha very much. An author of a certain locality was writing a book. The trash collector of the neighborhood accosted him on the street one day and tried to convince him that as between several different openings he had tried, he had certainly thrown away the best!

Bertha never failed to burn my discards daily.

Through the blocking out and juggling I achieve the memorizing. For the whole thing must stay with me every moment of the day and night. And unless it has been memorized, this is impossible.

While I am at the butcher's and he is cutting off the chops, I review the whole of a chunk. Often in these nooks and crannies of the day's activities I catch a fault or see that something makes a clutter; can be simplified or made more inevitable.

As you continue to snip and glue it becomes clearer and clearer just what has to be done. It almost writes itself, and when you reread it, it gives thrills, for the chapters are approaching a final form. You begin to see the shape of your thought on paper, chiseled out, like the profile on a cameo.

Each chapter is clipped together as the work goes on, and most of the pages have bits pinned to them, waiting until I can spare the time to rewrite the page. This is the work that can be done any time.

People ask me, Do you make your revision at the end when you've finished the book or as you go along?

If this process of juggling is what is meant by revision, it is an integral part of the creative work and is done many scores of times during the writing. This is not to say that it is not done at the end, too. The moment there has been a change—a cut, or transposition, or insertion, or elision, then there has to be rewriting, often of scores of pages.

Polishing goes on all the time. This is what we learn at school in English classes: punctuation, wording, phrasing, balance of sentences, paragraphing, composition.

The free writing and juggling have to be done to every part *as a unit;* every chapter, every chunk, every section, and finally to the book. And when this is done to the larger units, it almost invariably changes the balance of the smaller, and they have to be done again.

As to whether or not I am peculiar in my working methods or whether most writers go through these same processes, I think they do. The work I did on U.S. 30 certainly has to be done; also the free writing and juggling. But perhaps most writers rely more on memory than I do and less on notes.

For my own peace of mind, I could almost say my own sanity, I have had to protect myself against the barrage of the bits and of all the other ideas and chunks. A writer really lays himself open to a fearful torture.

I can put the sponge across the slate. I have deliberately taught myself to do this. Whole worlds are swept into oblivion. Sometimes I have a faint memory. . . . Wasn't there something good there? Something I ought not to forget? But it is gone. Therefore my bursting notebooks. Therefore my panic when ideas start running away from me. One chases another, I have found. Get a new idea and a dozen of yesterday vanish if they are not pinned down.

Twenty-two

I BEGAN *The Wyngate Children* with enthusiasm. I identified myself with my little heroine so completely that a critic was to say (and again it was Sterling North) ". . . the most appealing character is Jennifer, an ugly, lonesome little brat. The parts about her are written with the skill that one usually associates with the best kind of autobiography."

But in truth I was all of the children. Every author could make a dozen characters out of his single self. Every life has enough episodes and adventures to supply a whole group of fictional people.

It was I who played fifths all afternoon; who was asked to "play it big" (Reese asking me); who had the soprano voice of Cherry and was wanted for choir solos; who was dragged by the galloping horse (my pony, at Deercreek); who was caught in the rip tide; who had my tonsils sliced out without anesthetic; to whom was sung *"Ackieras Montagnas"* (but not by my mother—I had no mother); who put my little blue chair in the closet because I was going to hell; to whom the woman confessed for five hours.

It was a case of the old doggerel: Elizabeth, Liza, Betsy, and Bess, all went out to hunt a bird's nest. They found a bird's nest with four eggs in it, they each took one; three eggs were left.

The fiction writer, then, deals himself out to his group of characters and sets the episodes into a smooth context.

I have spoken of my hot mind and cold mind, but not yet of my "warning bell."

I have found that way down deep within me, a bell hangs. A warning bell. I don't always heed it because there's too much to worry about all the time. One is always skirting danger. But at times it pulls me up short; and if I disregard it without discovering and conquering the difficulty, I begin to feel ill.

The bell rang frequently as I proceeded with *The Wyngate Children,* but I disregarded it. Beginnings are always difficult.

Then I began to feel as if I was pushing a heavy weight. But when I'm once fairly started, I thought, I'll get up a real momentum, and it will begin to run along of itself. It was much too good a plan to be given up at the first bit of heavy going.

But I had pains everywhere and at last took to my bed, nauseated.

Taking to my bed when I'm doing a book does not mean always that I am actually ill. It means that every ounce of thought and energy, even that required to get up and dress, is needed for the effort. After all, when you are flat on your back, you are least impeded by the physical.

I began the book over innumerable times. I would get a new idea, new approach, which brought me out of bed with a leap. Tear up then; start over; rewrite; re-create; soar again. But every flight ended in a crash.

I was subjected, actually, to one serious shock after the other. I felt so dreadful, looked so dreadful, I sometimes thought something serious must be the matter with me. Should I send for Fran Williams?

What the warning bell kept telling me was that my heroine, Jennifer, was not carrying the book. She couldn't. And I couldn't make her, no matter how hard I tried. (Even writing about this makes my hands begin to sweat.) She wasn't important enough. Nothing that happened in the book or was going to happen was important enough to write about.

What misled me, what kept me struggling, was that I well knew children *are* important, important enough for any number of books. All that they feel and everything that happens to them is important. And this was not only an intellectual premise; it was in me as a deeply felt conviction.

I should have known that a red herring had been drawn across the trail.

I am well acquainted with the classical red herring. It menaces every writer of fiction. Just allow the reader's attention to be drawn off down a side trail with a pricking up of ears. *What's this? Why! Look here, what's going to happen!* and never again will you get his eye on your principal characters. They will mouth their lines in vain in the foreground. No one will see them or hear them. Poor Jennifer!

The Wyngate Children was turning out to be just what Mark Haverford had feared—a lot of kids cutting up. Most

[146]

irritating to the reader, because what the reader would be thinking about was the "thunderous problem" of the elders. That was the red herring.

The three or four months that I worked on this book are terrible even to look back upon; the long soliloquies when I decided that I had mistaken my vocation; when I completely lost control of my material, my chaos, and it formed itself into clouds like bees swarming, filling every cranny of my mind with a dark confusion.

But I could not give up. It was such a good plan. Publishers stood ready to spend thousands on the promotion of *a new novel about children by the author of My Friend Flicka.* They all (for even Mark had at last yielded) agreed that it was a wonderful plan.

And every one of us was wrong. It was not a good plan. There was a flaw in it that doomed my efforts from the start, and for all these agonizing months I had been attempting the impossible.

For a family is a unit. I had created my Wyngate family, children and parents, as a unit. And organic. You could not taste part of it without tasting the whole; or divide it without injuring its vital organs.

I had divided it. Limb from limb, eye from eye, heart, liver, lights, and lungs, every vital part divided; half of it to be used in the present book, and half saved for the next. A good way to commit murder.

That had been the plan—with emphasis on holding back the adult problem; don't even hint of that. Introduce the whole family of course, but nothing about the breach between the parents.

I had been faithful to the plan. Nowhere was there a

[147]

mention of that breach or any action that suggested it. But it was between the lines, implicit in the actions, the characters of every member of the family. Would Joyce have been the same if she had not had those parents? Or Jennifer? Would the house have been the same? No. In tasting part of that family you tasted the whole.

Bartholomew towered behind Jennifer. That great shadow looming. . . . No wonder she had not been able to carry the book. No wonder she was boring and trifling and the whole book boring and trifling. The reader, from the first scene when Bart and Louise appeared (there was the red herring), was impatient to get at the real problem of this family and impatient at being put off.

If your reader gets impatient with you, you've lost him. He'll probably not finish the book.

So it was that the plan was fundamentally wrong.

I did not see this until considerably later, and it was Whit who pointed it out to me. I was too close to it. But I did see another fatal flaw. The book was ruining the character of my hero.

I have written at length about the difficulty I was having in getting Bart right. The reader now met him in his relation to Jennifer. Whimsical, loving, tender, indulgent, wise—an ideal Papa. But *that* was not the protagonist I had conceived! And if this book made him so (in some inexplicable way Jennifer made him so), then I would never be able to resurrect him for the next book.

I shadow-boxed with this impasse for a long time, debating whether different scenes of introduction might not perhaps save Bart's character and so the whole book and the next book. Sometimes a different angle—just a

[148]

little twist—and lo! here is a new path and one gets through the jungle after all!

I wrote it again and again. But when I would read it over the next morning, I would be aware of another of those terrible shocks, and would sit as if paralyzed.

I buried the book; pulled it out of the grave and began it again; buried it; pulled it out again. At last I wished it would stay buried.

It is hard for me to give up. So many lost causes have, in the end, not been lost just because of not giving up. I wondered if by any chance Whit would see any hope for it? Here, obviously, was an opportunity for my special editor to be of help to me.

But it was a difficult situation. I had no faith in it myself. Would not my disaffection (if I let him see it) inevitably affect him? Well then, don't let him see it. Just send it to him, go to him, and get his reaction.

It was about Easter time of 1950 that I did this.

In practicing his profession of editing Whit has no inhibitions. He holds nothing back. There is no petting, no effort to be tactful. He takes it for granted that when I am about to present a book to the public it is a help to me to suffer in advance the worst attack that can be made against it. And I agree. This is his value to me.

But it is hard to take—would be hard for any writer. In the book about Maxwell Perkins, editor, and Thomas Wolfe, author, when Perkins gave it as his opinion that an enormous section of Wolfe's book would have to be cut out, there was dead silence in that office for one hour, as those two men sat looking at each other. One can imagine what Wolfe was suffering. When I was working in the movies, I knew it to happen that a scenario writer lost consciousness under the strain of having her work torn to pieces in such a conference, and was carried out in a dead faint.

Though I have been toughened by experience, yet I was dizzy, as if crashes of thunder were playing around me. At the same time I felt enormous relief at the ending of doubt and indecision.

Of course Whit could not know this, and he continued in the face of my silence as though he thought he had to beat down opposition.

As the weight of the impossible book rolled off my back I marveled quite objectively at the variations he could so swiftly extemporize on the themes of *boring* and *trifling*. It was Jennifer, of course, who was boring and trifling. (Poor Jennifer—could you ever carry a book, Jennifer?)

Whit had not so far told me anything I didn't know. I waited, looking for the illumination that, usually, accompanies his thunder. At last came a dart. . . .

"When you write about the mature men and what they say, it's good. Your theme of a clergyman who cannot reconcile his inner, spiritual life with his outer, is good." This was valuable reassurance.

"We're all through with *Little Women* and books like that."

This was not so valuable. In fact, he immediately reversed himself by saying, "But I'm crazy about the three levels."

He meant the three love affairs of my "little women"— Joyce and Jennifer, and the larger affair of their mother. He wanted Jennifer a year or two older so she could better play the part of precocious child just moving into adolescence. He felt there were too many children. Cut out the two boys, Cecil and Runo. It was really the girls' story.

This was the way he saw it. Since he is creative himself, it is impossible for him not to seize those elements he prefers and envision the story as he would write it. He always does this and I expect it, but that is not the kind of help I need, and I just wait for him to get through. What I like is swift and complete demolition. Clear the ground for me. Then leave the rebuilding to me.

I had never told Whit much about Runo, what a character I hoped he would turn out to be, far more important than the girls; and that toward the end of the book his little hand would turn out to be the mighty hand of God. (You can't really put a thing like that into spoken words— it would sound quite unreal.) Nor had I told him much about Cecil, who was the idol of his mother; or that her superstitious dread that something bad would happen to him began to have an effect on her character. That, too, was too hazy to talk about.

It was not until I was leaving and we were standing at the door and Whit had somewhat got over his disappointment (for I think the loss of this book was a blow to him too) and was beginning to understand my own attitude about it, that he said as a sort of afterthought, "And of course, in these hundred pages the breach between the parents is not concealed at all. It's perfectly apparent."

As I drove from New York to Tyrawley on the Merritt Parkway, it was this last remark, a postscript, that illuminated the whole difficulty. Although I had seen many flaws in the book, this one fundamental flaw I had failed to see; and now I knew why the bell had tolled so warningly all the time; and I exclaimed aloud, "Why, of course! Now I see! It just couldn't be done! The plan was impossible from the start!"

The book would stay in its grave now. I was grateful to Whit for giving it its quietus, and I began to feel the deep, delicious fatigue that surely meant I would be able to rest, to forget this, even to sleep without dreams.

I wrote Lippincott telling of the demise of *The Wyngate Children;* of my conference with Whit; that he had helped me bury it; that "as far as I am concerned he has earned his thousand-dollar fee already." That I was going back to the original book as I had at first conceived it.

Mark Haverford was at this time in Bermuda, sailing his yacht in the big race. Frank was just leaving for his vacation. So it devolved upon Leigh, in April, 1950, to write me the letter of condolence; sympathizing, encouraging, congratulating me on being at last on the right track and all set to go.

Twenty-three

May 2, 1950

. . . awfully depleted and drained . . . trying to think how to get energy when it's gone . . . went to piano and improvised . . . feel better . . . strength is gathering in me. . . . I wondered about the power of the body to respond to the right stimulus. . . . This is in the book, interesting I think . . . the clinic, Justin Hughes the doctor . . . the glands pour out hormones and the body is acted upon and performs magically all along the line. . . . How to give the necessary fillip to the glands? I have just done it with music . . . definitely feel quite different and much better . . . it could be done by anything: weather, view, a star, a cloud, a face, a voice, a word. . . .

Kim had a very bad fight that spring. A large black and white Dalmatian came boldly into the Tyrawley driveway and right up to the house. It looked as though it was going to be a fight to the death.

But they were too evenly matched. Neither one could kill the other, and they kept on, ignoring commands, blows, the water hose, until they couldn't move.

Kim was terribly slashed, drenched in blood, but no bones were broken.

He was so nervous that if I left him for a moment he began to cry. He habitually slept in the basement, and I upstairs. As a concession to his honorable wounds I allowed him, for a few nights, to sleep on the floor beside my bed, and Erik Olsen came over to carry him up and down the stairs.

Knowing Kim, he brought with him a bandage that he intended winding around Kim's muzzle before lifting him. But by this time I had bought a leather muzzle for Kim as well as ten thousand dollars' worth of liability insurance.

I do not think either muzzle or bandage would have been needed on that occasion, for Kim knew what was being done for him, and relaxed himself upon that big Swedish chest with gratitude.

I invited the Du Chenes up for a visit.

Allie and I drove all over the countryside visiting antique shops while Aroldo lay on the sofa in the living room with a black bandage over his eyes.

When we got back, we asked him if he had rested. "Not only rested, I have had a spiritual recharging."

He had the ability to make himself empty to receive the recharging. He becomes negative. Something positive flows in.

I needed recharging too.

... Aroldo says Kim has an interior quality ... one hears that said of people, spiritual people, saints ... but a dog? Yet there is something strange in Kim ... he stands in the middle of the room ... motionless ... head slightly lowered, listening acutely ... aware as an animal is not supposed to be. ...

Aroldo says Kim's eyes are slightly insane . . . well, perhaps. . . .

It is one of my rules never to count the cost of work or time or effort or even health, provided I acquire one good building block for the final structure of the book.

The Wyngate Children was not a dead loss. Jennifer, as a character, went into *The Son of Adam Wyngate* almost *in toto.* She was no longer boring and trifling. In fact, not only Sterling North but most of the critics commented favorably upon her. And critics are important. If the financial success of an author depends on the public, his prestige, to a great extent, depends on the critics. And I think they are very fair.

All the same, energy is not infinite, nor time. I am too profligate; I should not always be looking down bypaths, wondering what conflagrations might be starting over there.

Yet now, once again, I did just that.

The warning bell tolled.

I paid no attention.

I can really blame this diversion on Whit. For before I talked to him I was ready to toss away the organist and cadet and the romance of the two girls. After that remark of Whit's—*I'm crazy about the three levels*—there they were again. I was going to lift them bodily out of *The Wyngate Children* and put them into *The Son of Adam Wyngate.* For if Whit liked them, wouldn't others? Of course they would. I liked them myself. I was crazy about them.

My bell tolled loudly. *It can't be done. There wouldn't*

be room enough for it the way you write even in a book of a thousand pages.

We'll try it anyway and see what happens. . . .

You'll be sorry. You ought to know by this time that you write the single-line story.

I wanted to abandon the difficult techniques I had learned; techniques of shape and form; and rhythm and timing; and emphasis and accent; all that subtle differentiation of preparatory, climactic, and windup writing. And this in spite of the service they had rendered me.

I knew that many of the greatest novels had been written without reference to any rigid dramatic form. Why should not mine? I had a fluent pen—why not just let the words pour? And hope to have it come out pleasant and readable?

This was not merely a break for freedom as I described it in an earlier chapter, or laziness either. What knowledge I have, I have acquired by the process of trial and error, always experimenting and exploring. It would hardly be true to type for me to ignore a bypath.

So now I was going to do a triple-line story instead of single line; episodic rather than accumulative (movie terms); a discursive rather than dramatically constructed book.

I had masses of material ready to put into it, and I started in with vigor, though not with a particularly firm idea that what I was writing would be final. There was a day of reckoning ahead. But there always is that. I would do the reckoning when the time came for it; meanwhile I would not look down into those final depths, but in a more superficial manner, get onto numbered pages this story—these three stories—which by now I knew so well.

What I was unaware of at the time (it is easier to see such things at a remove of several years) was that I was still using the same slide rule to measure by; indeed I had no other. Was a page bad and to be torn up and done over? What law commanded this? To what pattern did the page not conform? To those same patterns, measured by those same rules, which had always been my guides; my sure guides; and my only guides.

They still were my only guides.

The telephone call came through from London late one night. It was from Kent. I heard him say,

"He's got ten little fingers . . . and ten little toes. . . ."

They had decided that if it was a boy the name should be of Kent's family; if a girl, of Deirdre's. But Kent could not, at this delirious moment, remember the family names.

So, over the transoceanic telephone, I recited the family names, racking my brains for the most distinguished, famous, or romantic characters.

We continued this hunt nightly by telephone until the porter at Kent's London club said, "Haven't you got that baby named yet?"

He was finally named Jonathan and christened at the church in Thornhill near Deirdre's Yorkshire home.

So, I thought, two young people get themselves married; they become parents; there is a little new creature in the world named Jonathan—all before I have been able to make more than the beginning of my particular creation. . . .

But the work was going well. I scanned one day and was quite seized by the interest of the girls' romances. There were corrections to make, but of a superficial kind; they did not bite down deep into the structure.

I made the corrections and listed them. I pinned the scrap of paper up on my board, a perpetual finger uplifted admonishing me; a perpetual frown bending down upon me. . . .

Too much author.

Too much reflection.

Too much all at once.

Too much thought stream.

Too academic and literary.

Too much in the minds of the characters.

Too much exposition.

Too much retrospect in a cold cut.

Too much . . . too much . . . too much. . . .

Twenty-four

AT EVERY step of the way the story has to be, in the beginning, disentangled from many other stories.

In actual life, you could say, each person lives his story through from birth to death, and it seems straight and simple, quite separated from the lives he did not live. But juxtaposed to that story, entangled with it, are all those other stories which he might have lived but did not. And it's a close line sometimes. . . . *Heavens! If I had done that. . . . Or, If I only had not done this. . . .*

Less than the toss of a coin divides the life he lived from the life he did not live—that had no being whatsoever.

Just so in fiction. The author has at every step of the way to disentangle what actually (in the finished book) does happen, from all those other things that might have happened.

And are they many—those other might-have-been stories?

They are legion. And, in their separate parts, there is nothing to distinguish them to the eyes of the author from the true.

[159]

If you had many pieces of yarn tangled together, you could easily disentangle them provided they were of different colors. But if they were not . . .

Or, if someone showed you a great tub of pearls, telling you that it contained certain ones of an exact shade and shape that, properly put together, would make a flawless string—but that there were also pearls there that would make other strings, not quite so flawless but still fine—and still others only fit to be thrown away—and that it was your job to select the pearls that would make that flawless string and then make it, grading it perfectly . . .

It amused me sometimes to sit at my typewriter with my hands in my lap, staring out the window, thinking up these analogies.

I remembered a toy that I had as a child: a pad of paper about two inches square, on each page a picture. Flip them quickly through from first to last and you see a moving picture, perhaps a horse race. Suppose you had a score of such gadgets, or a hundred. And in each one, though the jockeys are the same, and the horses, yet it is a different race. And suppose the toys had been taken apart, so that every tiny picture was detached from the others; and all these pictures were tossed in a pile together, all scrambled up; and it was your job to pick out of this mass the pictures that—properly put together—would make just one race—the best, most exciting, most effective race of all!

But there are clues. An author has clues. A dog would pick the right glove out of a pile of gloves by a sense of smell. It is something like that. The author can pick out the right scene by a sort of sense of smell.

How much should be considered a day's work?

A friend of mine began to write short stories when she was about twenty-two and for thirty years never failed to sell one.

She did not revise and seldom wrote anything twice. She did all that in her head. She wrote very slowly in longhand, with pauses—sometimes a half-hour pause. She limited herself to twenty-five hundred words a day. In typing, that would be about eight pages of double spacing, and it is a great deal. When it was done, she handed it to her secretary and never saw it again herself. The secretary would type it, mail it to the agent, and there would come, in due time, the note from the agent and the check.

When I was writing *My Friend Flicka,* Whit Burnett told me of another author in whose work he was interested. He said she had a daytime job and wrote at night, contenting herself with just three pages.

I thought, three a day, that's ninety a month. In four months, three hundred and sixty pages—a complete novel! Had she written a complete novel in four months? But when I asked him how long she had been working on this book, he answered, "Six years."

So I saw that with her, as with me, a hundred pages of work lay behind the one finished page.

I had thought it a wise rule, and applied it to my own working habits. I would never fret, when the going was slow and difficult, if I did three pages in a day.

Now, however, I was doing much more than that.

I pinned up some questions on my board.

What about Ramsey? Should he be introduced in person or a flashback?

I took down the question, wrote the answer and pinned that up instead.

Introduce Ramsey in flashback ... don't want him to be particularly vivid.

I wrote another question and pinned it up.

What kind of a man is Ramsey?

This still baffled me. I forbade myself to go on with any other work until I had mastered this character. I had been procrastinating about him long enough.

... simply cannot understand this man. ... I'm shirking him, that's the truth of it. ... The other day I wrote that I would show him in flashbacks only because I didn't want to make him vivid and important. ... Why? WHY? for pity's sake? Why is the man who wrecks your life not vivid to you? Why can he not be there right in the present moment in front of you, his eyes locked in yours? Precipitating the first-class scene in first-class presentation—such a scene as when the two white stallions fought in *Thunderhead?*
But I can't bear to bring him in like that. ... After all, the true conflict in this book is between Bart and his wife. ... But what sort of soul is this Ramsey?

With reluctance I put my mind on Ramsey. I had once been given a screen assignment to make an adaptation of a magazine story entitled *There Are No Villains.*
This is just what I feared. Think about Ramsey deeply enough, and his villainy would ooze away, and he would

turn into just one more suffering, sinning human, and you would be sorry for him. I didn't want my readers to be sorry for him.

I had been reading a recently published book (very fine) called *My Six Convicts*. I got this book to help me study villains. Surely in a penetentiary full of convicts there would be villains enough; but alas!—not one you could really hate; though they killed freely; conspired against the law; wreaked their vengeance without mercy.

A very good friend of mine was the Public Defender of Connecticut. I knew he spent many hours talking with his clients in the jail. He would surely be able to describe the true psychology of a villain. But when I asked him, he laughed.

"Why, Mary, there aren't any! Not one but can convince you that he's just playing in hard luck. And many of them are!"

All the same, I knew that there were good souls, and better and best. And there were bad and worse and worst.

. . . now I'm getting somewhere. . . . How bad do I want Ramsey to be? Not the worst . . . no . . . but awfully bad. Must hate him . . . how would I ever know about such a one . . . never met one. . . . I keep away from people I can't like. . . .

I racked my brains to discover that degree of incarnated evil in anyone I had ever known, and failed. The most I could say was that I had known good people who did bad things.

Well then, look in books, in plays, newspaper articles, history, court trials. Yes, here were horrible villains. Then must I use this sort of secondhand data out of which to

[163]

construct the character of my villain? This did not altogether satisfy me. Get closer to him then. Analyze him. Exactly what sort of villain was he? What sins? Cruelty perhaps? Though so many people are cruel. Sadistic? That didn't seem bad enough either. Selfish? Nearly everyone is selfish in one way or another or at certain times of his life. . . .

. . . sleeping badly . . . awful dreams . . . wake up and snatch paper and scribble notes . . . papers accumulating . . . afraid to throw anything away . . . keep examining them . . . *awful.* . . .

. . . today revised, reclassified all I did this past week. . . . Went through my notes for the next chunk . . . arranged them, pinned bunches together . . . jotted down some new ones . . . wrote five new pages. . . .

I've always thought of Ramsey as a type, too good-looking, too sought after, particularly by women . . . just spoiled the way fruit turns rotten and smells . . . like something in which putrefaction has set in . . . or, a building block, or nail, or board that has been damaged and is now useless and is tossed away—spoiled in that sense. He's just no good any more . . . not good for anything. . . .

. . . lots of such men around . . . he's almost a cliché . . . handsome and gifted young men and women too early successful so that all that comes after in life is a disappointment, a gradual and bitter loss of treasures he thought he held by divine right. . . . They take it out on everyone else. . . . But if it's a woman, she gets a discipline from nature that a man doesn't get . . . so she's corrected . . . she becomes a mother . . . it changes her . . . changed Louise . . . she's better than Ramsey . . . Ramsey married for money. . . .

[164]

I was gradually getting closer to Ramsey. I saw his faults, his sins. The sins of the frustrated egomaniac. Excessive aggressiveness; cruelty; ruthlessness; coldheartedness; envy; contempt for the gentle and good (Bart); incapacity for love; cold and careless lustfulness.

It never became easy for me to write about Ramsey. The moment his name appeared on a sheet of paper, I was tense. But I was no longer shirking him. I had come to grips with him, and as a consequence, he had come alive for me.

He moved through his scenes easily; he acted with spontaneity, broke into laughter or scorn; I could see his face, and the expressions that played across it.

And I could see that he added the tension of danger to the story.

Twenty-five

Now THAT I was embarked on what I kept trying to think was the real and the final version of the book, I began to consider style and finish.

As regards style, screen writing is the worst training in the world.

Screen writing is elaborate and detailed stage directions.

It is the book of plans and specifications that an architect gives to the builder.

A scenario is full of lists of objects and props and exactly pictured locations. It must be clear. Repeat the same word wherever necessary for precision. The balanced sentence or paragraph is of no importance. Nor is the artistic gem of description. For who will see it? It is for the cameraman, the director, the actor to make the pictures.

The use of the present tense gives a peculiarly low-brow effect. *Bill smashes Harry in the face*. Clichés are fine. Old friends. Really better than original wordings.

Dialogue is important. Dramatic construction is important. And a good story line. But these are not style.

Grammar is not important. Many of those who read

and pass on your scenario will not know good grammar from bad; you must only make yourself clear.

Dots and dashes pass for punctuation and serve quite as well—easier to read too.

An author could write for the screen for twenty-five years and become successful and famous yet never develop any style; whereas if he studies and practices literature and writing in other fields, he is likely to get a finished and individual style quite soon.

Perhaps, in the matter of grammar, book publishers have been infected by the screen; for many of them make no objection when an omniscient author writes, "It don't," or "She ain't," or "John was laying on the bed." I object to this, for I have a passion for syntax. As a child I was fascinated by Latin, because by means of the complicated syntax, so much could be said in so few words.

But in the matter of punctuation, there is a new freedom too. And this I do like, because I feel the old symbols to have been inadequate.

. . . I've been wondering about the use of the dash in really good modern books . . . just went to my library to look . . . Faulkner, Hemingway, Ullman, Mailer all use it in new ways . . . I myself use it as a modified exclamation. For instance, *He reached the cliff and stood there looking out over the ocean— wonderful—wonderful—* This gives just that degree of breathlessness which is right . . . an exclamation point would make it ridiculous, a comma or semicolon too flat. . . .

Moreover, today, writing is supposed to mirror thought more closely. . . . Thought is not punctuated. . . . I remember Cousin Mabel, who used to punctuate her thought and everything that came out of her mouth! (Yes, truly, an exclamation

[167]

mark for that!) I was only a little girl but I was so amazed, used to stare at her so steadily, I was reprimanded for rudeness.

People break their thoughts off unfinished . . . say *thingamajig,* or *you know what I mean* or wave their hands. . . . Well then, should not authors do the same? Instead of the old-fashioned way as Cousin Mabel did of carefully finishing every thought and tucking it in neatly with commas and periods—yes, just wave hands (dashes?).

Really, thought so seldom ends . . . is so nearly always suspended . . . just left hanging in the air dash dash dash

Perhaps the worst blight Hollywood put upon me was the necessity of dealing with trashy material, or with good material in a trashy way. Often my best writing was turned down and I was forced to compromise.

A writer in Hollywood has only limited power. After the script is finished the director can change it, or another writer can be called in, unbeknownst to the first, to rewrite.

I cannot blame the director for making whatever changes he feels desirable, for he has the final responsibility. If he cannot wholly understand and accept what the script writer has set down for him to do, he must change it until he can. Otherwise he could not put his heart into his direction.

Close collaboration between writer and director would be the answer, and there are some such teams, but usually both are hired separately by the production manager and thrust upon each other. They can be fired or replaced according to his will.

This was a formidable danger surrounding and influencing me all the time, particularly as I was not conscious of it as a danger to my writing. I accepted conditions as they were, and had no thought of preserving or training any literary skills I possessed for future use in a different field.

A danger I soon became more conscious of was my own childlike love of an exciting story.

In the movies, suspense was overdone. True. Yet suspense is good; it holds you. In a book it makes you turn the pages. Besides, it is the truth. There is much suspense in life. But to reproduce it in fiction entails contrivance; and sometimes at the cost of veracity and rhythm. The alternating shots of pursued and pursuer on the screen that we have all become so familiar with no longer have any suspense whatsoever. They are just trite and silly. This is still a difficulty for me: the urgency to do—the dread of overdoing. I often find myself trying to get suspense *out* of scenes instead of putting it *in*.

Another Hollywood blight was that idea that one must create for an audience aged twelve.

I never did accept this, and so got no damage from it. That is, I never accepted the sentimentality, trashiness, obviousness, or triteness that had become traditional Hollywood. One could find, I thought, a common ground.

I remember the critic who said of Tchaikovsky that in his music little tunes kept breaking through.

Twelve-year-olds like those tunes.

And I know a Leipzig Doctor of Music who admired a little melody, as short and simple and clear as *Stille Nacht*—when half a dozen other savants scoffed at it. Twelve-year-olds would have liked that too.

It is not only Hollywood that holds the idea that moving picture audiences must be written down to. Many established eastern authors go to California, not with any idea of getting their best work onto the screen, or as much of it as is possible, but all set to write trash and sell it.

I remember when a New York playwright had a good laugh at me. He was supervising a picture for Cecil De Mille, and I was the screen writer assigned to his unit. "Miss O'Hara! Don't take it so seriously! This is pictures, Miss O'Hara! Moving pictures!"

He was laughing because I had demurred at writing scenes that would show a man in two places at once.

My reply was to ask Mr. De Mille to be released from my contract. Some time later, I happened to be seated, at a dinner party, beside C. B. De Mille's older brother, William. And he asked me why I had left C. B.'s studio. I told him, "Because I was assigned to E—— H——'s unit. And E—— H—— does not mind a man being in two places at once."

"Or even three!" agreed William with considerable relish.

It is so large a question—whether or not the artist must write down to his audience—that I cannot answer it except for myself. I always sought those emotions and attitudes that are common to all human beings, whether educated or not. Even a moron can feel despair or rise to heights of courageous sacrifice.

I've read over everything I've written . . . it's a lot . . . the writing has been going well, that is, fluently . . . it's awfully good stuff . . . awfully good really but I'm not sure . . . not sure . . . seems to go on and on . . . such a lot more in my head and in my notebooks. . . . Don't ever seem to make a dent in it. . . . How many pages could there be in a book, even a big book? . . . It ought, somehow, to be related in its length to its mass. . . . What do I mean? . . . I'm blocking out the first chunk of section two now. . . . First, disentangle the plot steps. There are always more than you think . . . write each single one, a single sentence on separate slips of paper. Pin them on the board in a certain order. Study them, particularly the order of them. Try a different order. Juggle them. Decide on *hierarchy* of these plot steps. . . .

I kept on writing all summer without any change in my plan; or my hopes.

Early in October Kent and Deirdre and Jonathan embarked on a troop transport and headed for this country. Kent's foreign duty was over; he had been assigned to Wright Field, Dayton, Ohio.

They were to spend a month with me first, at Tyrawley, and on a cold October day I met the ship in the Brooklyn Navy Yard.

With what speed I turned into an irate grandmother! (I had determined *never* to do this.) I saw Kent bringing the baby down the gangplank in a little English carry-cot, a small basket swung in a strong webbing by which it can be grasped.

They had no sooner got to the dock and set the basket down than they began stripping off the baby's sweater and unwinding his blankets, because the little bare-armed frock was more becoming!

Kent and Deirdre and I, be it known, were all done up in sweaters and woolens against the sharp October wind. The baby, they told me, was not to be coddled in the steam-heated American way. He was to be brought up tough and hardy.

Helplessly I stood and guarded the basket while Kent and Deirdre went off to attend to luggage; and half a dozen stevedores and coal heavers gathered around me, snapping their fingers at the baby, and demanding angrily of me why his head was bare on such a day!

I quite agreed with them.

"If that was *my* baby!"

"Where's his mother?"

"Say—here's my cap—"

Twenty-six

Nov. 30, 1950

... discouragement autointoxicates you ... It is a poison ... I fall asleep all the time ... well, go back ... ask the fundamental questions again. ...

1) Is this a story worth writing? Yes.
2) Can you do it? No reason why I cannot.
3) Can you do Bartholomew? Why not? I know his thoughts.

It always lifted me and set me at my task with fresh courage.

What's worrying you then?
I think it's Bart ... all these *girls* around him ... he's not coming out right ... girls, girls girls ... the organist and the cadet. ... Bart's lost ... the book's about Jennifer and Joyce. ...

I tried to right myself from the violent tossing, telling myself that learning is always hard. This was new for me, writing in this kind of ambling, discursive fashion about so many things at once.

... I've read it all over and the whole thing is a failure. It's good in its separate parts, its characters, and ... I feel all the time ... its promise.... *It's going to be good* ... but when? Dozens, scores, hundreds of pages done ... heaven knows how much I've got clipped together into chapters but still it is several separate stories instead of one.... It's Bart's and Joyce's and Jennifer's and I've no sooner hit the right pace to prepare for climactic action along one story line than I have to leave it to go to another ... and then the long preparation and building up on *that* line ... then cutting away from that and back to the other, only to find that the suspense you took so long to build has snapped ... and you begin a scene that ought to be climactic, and you write it as if it was a climax, and then you see it isn't ... it's just flat and silly and ridiculous....

The bulk and mass of the written chapters oppressed me and I began to feel as if I was being submerged.

Life took on a nightmare quality.

... don't know what to do ... I'm losing control of my material as I did before ... it seems as if it isn't in the desk any more ... it's all over my room ... crowding my head ... lost its order ... perhaps it's just that I'm distracted having Kent and Deirdre and the baby here.... My mind is full of them. ... I don't want to work.... I've been trying to keep my usual early morning hours for writing but what's the use? ... I think I'm stale....

Dec. 10, 1950

... but now that they've gone, still I can't work ... can't begin ... it feels as if I was trying to lift a mountain and set it on my back again....

Dec. 11

... so dead tired ... almost a coma ... one can't write in such a state....

Now I've read it all through again . . . all of it . . . *all of it from start to finish* . . . it's no good. *No good . . . NO GOOD. . . .*

I just can't believe this. . . .

Don't I know anything at all? . . .

. . . beginning to feel very peculiar . . . as if I was really coming down with something this time. . . . There's a lot of flu around . . . could that be it? . . . Certainly my brain's not working the way it ought to. . . .

. . . WHAT'S THE MATTER WITH THIS BOOK!

Christmas came and went. I stopped trying to work. I paid visits. Went to New York, to Dayton. And returned.

Every time I returned I would go to my writing room and stand looking at my desk. Just stand leaning against the wall looking at it. I couldn't sit down.

. . . if you're stuck, never look forward, never try to go forward . . . look back . . . you've gone wrong somewhere. . . .

I've done two hundred and twenty pages of this book . . . none of it any good. . . .

My temperature went up, and I gave in and went to bed. I took an armful of books on writing with me: Maugham, Henry James, Edward J. O'Brien, Katherine Mansfield, Maxwell Perkins, Willa Cather, Vincent McHugh. I propped myself up with pillows, but then, instead of taking a book, got my typewriter and set it across my knees.

... fundamental things wrong ... things that should have been done and done right before I began the book ... but what does that matter? One could say now that I have not begun the book yet (Oh, my God—after two years!). Yes ... apparently I have just been mulling over my material ... begin over then ... go back to those questions. ...

1) Is this book worth doing? *Yes. YES!*
2) Can I do it? *Yes I can!*
3) What's your story, Mary? *About this mystic. ...*

I knew the thumbnail synopsis by heart. It had been hanging before my eyes for a year. But I climbed out of bed and went to my writing room and pulled out the thumbtack and took the little slip of paper—about as big as a post card—back to bed with me.

Here was my story. Here was my book.

And there was not a word in it about the romances of Joyce and Jennifer. Their names were not even in it.

They were just two red herrings.

And so at last I gave up on book three.

Twenty-seven

I was now to experience that extraordinary lightening of the heart that comes when an encumbering weight has been removed. But the first thing it did was put me to sleep.

There, covered with the typewriter, manuscript chapters, and the many books on how to write a novel, I slept for hours.

I was ill for several weeks that time. It was delicious.

With the dropping of the romances of the two girls and their swains, the road lay clear ahead of me, a single-line story, and I had all the guides to keep me straight upon it; but I had not, at that time, much certainty about anything. My brain refused to work. I thought it was probable that I could not write novels, and I was rather relieved about it. I could see that there were very pleasant aspects to failure.

But as I emerged from the agreeable nothingness of fever and failure I found myself quite frequently thinking about that thumbnail synopsis.

One day I got up from my bed, rummaged around

among the papers in my writing room until I found it, and then sat down at my desk, holding it in my two hands, studying it. I did not go back to bed again.

A study of sacred and profane love. Samuel Wyngate, mystic; that portion of his life which comprises his trial and emergence (death and rebirth theme). He is an Interior Soul, unsuited to large city parish and family responsibilities. Great and jealous love of Louise, his charming and flighty wife. He is being crushed and borne down but could stand up under it except for his weak point—excessive love of his wife. Story focuses on Ramsey, his older brother with whom Louise has had an affair. She has had others too. When Samuel discovers in himself hatred first for Ramsey, then Louise, he goes to pieces; can no longer take Communion, administer the Sacraments, preach, or keep his church.

Well—here was the story of his trial but not his emergence. How was he to emerge? I put paper into the typewriter and wrote quickly:

Men are given directions for saving themselves; and if they obey, as Bart does, and suffer through it as Job did, they do emerge.
The end is not necessarily that Louise reforms and will thereafter never again stray (for who could trust her?) or that Bart regains his reason, fame, his parish; but that his heart is cleansed.

I tacked this paragraph on my board below the other. The thumbnail synopsis was now complete. It told the whole story. I could send it to Lippincott. It could be sent out as an advance notice of the book.

I got thinking about that emergence. It was a subtle

thing. Circumstances had driven Bartholomew crazy (for I had known for some time he would have a mental collapse). Circumstances did not change much, and yet he recovers. How and why?

This part of the book must be so true, so utterly lifelike and inevitable, it must be *what naturally would happen.*

There would be that girl, the nurse, Kristy, who loved him; and he loved her; long ago he had done for her, in a way, by confidence and stanch friendship, what she was now to do for him. (I never had any trouble with this angelic character—perhaps everyone knows such a one.) But it would not be a love affair in the ordinary sense.

I had actually made a very exact abstract outline of it in that quickly written thumbnail paragraph.

I now began to analyze and dissect every sentence of it, considering each separately.

Men are given directions for saving themselves; and if they obey—Bart does obey, of course. He is incapable of doing otherwise. And the first act of obedience is the honest self-searching and the discovery of the hatred in his own heart. His longing to be cleansed of it is prayer. Then confession, which he expressed in his talk with Quentin Gerrity; confessed not only the hating of his wife but disobedience to God, for "against Thee and Thee only have I sinned. (Is not every sin against God?) To continue, *if they suffer through it as Job did.* Bart did suffer. Those scenes of his great suffering were already, many of them, on paper.

Faith, obedience, confession, suffering, prayer—not forgetting the prayers of those who loved him as well as his own; Gerrity said he would pray for his cleansing.

Standing thus, on the rock, how could Bart fail to emerge? But it would be a gradual thing; slow; little by little.

What naturally would happen is, in life, quite often very undramatic. Unbearable situations are somehow eased though they seem little changed. Now they can, somehow, be borne, where before they could not. Something that would break a man if he were friendless can easily be endured if a friend appears to stand by.

And for Bart there would be Kristy.

So my abstract was true and right.

Here were the deep waters, the ground swell rising and thrusting into a comber. Now for that wind to lash and drive it until the line of foam springs out on the crest, and there is the story line, one concrete scene after the other unfolding. I saw how they would fall into place simply and easily and rightly; how neatly they would link themselves into continuity.

Rolling along . . . I let my mind stream forward. And, remarkable to say, I seemed to be all there again, with all the swiftness and enthusiasm necessary to carry me along to the end.

I knew I was back on the rails. A single-line dramatic story. The only kind I know how to write.

How I wished, then, that I could have had several pairs of hands so that I could have begun at part two, Bart's collapse and emergence, all now so fresh and pressing (and this, of course, was the Marshlands part—here Ramsey would do his worst—I was ready for Ramsey, too) and at the same time begin at the beginning and do the complete rewrite on that, the opening and all the Brooklyn part.

I did, in fact, try to write both parts at once, making extensive notes for the last half, keeping it all fresh in my mind, while I rushed through the new chapters for the beginning.

Away with the girls!

It was exhilarating to realize how heavy an encumbrance had been removed from the book.

There was, however, one small cloud in my sky. I could not bring myself to like the Joyce-Ramsey relationship, and yet I accepted the fact that it must be there. Why else was Joyce in the book? This subsidiary story line was not apart and separate from the main story line as the girls' romances had been; this was truly interlocked with the Bart-Louise problem.

But I refused to be downhearted. I took heart of hope. Other problems had, one by one, been solved. This one would too. If I needed another miracle, it would come.

This, now, was book four I was beginning.

On January 27, I wrote to Whit:

... the parallel stories of Joyce and Jennifer never inextricably united with their father's story and are therefore, to me, an incurable disunity. ...

and I enclosed the thumbnail synopsis, complete with emergence. I received a nice reply:

... an acknowledgment of your letter in which for the first time, I believe, the singleness of purpose and story line has been put on paper where, I must say, it looks good. ... I honestly believe you have boiled away all the volatile elements and just the meat is left. It should go better with you now and there should be no lack of confidence in how you can handle it . . . it should have a hungry public. . . . Maturity is one of the things this age is growing into, or trying to. . . .

Whit thus reversed himself. It was one of the reasons for my confidence in him that it never troubled him to plunge wholeheartedly in one direction and then in the opposite. He is absolutely sincere. Besides, on such a point as this, the decision must be the author's, and he would be the first to say so.

I wrote Lippincott; told them I had made some simplifications in the story line that I thought would quicken my pace to the finish and asked them how they would like the title *When Doth Sorrow First Approach?*

I enclosed the thumbnail synopsis.

Twenty-eight

I WAS interested in this title because of the way big things grow out of little things.

First, a vast, meaningless, complicated web of human thought and action, and then within the strands of that diaphanous web, the lines of a tragic pattern gradually appear; the large happenings precipitated by the small.

For instance, a casual and accidental glance out the window . . . and if you had not taken it, you wouldn't have seen such and such, or given the alarm, or fallen downstairs and broken your back and blighted the lives of your children forever after.

Or, when you have dressed, you go back into your room to change your blue handkerchief for a pink . . . and that retardation of a minute or two changes every contact you make that morning, and some tragedy (or joy) ensues that would not have, had you gone out with the blue.

The large and important plot steps I had pretty well determined on when I evolved my theme and thumbnail synopsis. But the story itself cannot be written or even begun in continuity until there stand out in it those small

[183]

things that will start the chain of events that end in the large things.

The finding of these small things is arduous work. They grow out of character. It is only as you dwell on one character after the other and he comes more and more to life and develops this or that trait or habit that he begins in a natural and spontaneous way to do the sort of thing you are looking for.

So, first decide on the large plot steps.

Then work on the characters.

Then watch your characters in action so that you can see and pounce upon the small things that can move the plot.

Such as Bart forgetting the notes of his sermon.

Ramsey knowing just where Louise had left her evening wrap and Bart's observing this.

The oversight about the lamp switch.

Louise leaving her book in the garden.

The sound of Louise's bangles.

In my very first session with Whit, when I had shown him the exposition I also showed him a scrap of a scene I had written, Jennifer finding the big key under the scarves in her mother's bureau drawer.

He demanded, "What's this going to be about the key?"

"I haven't any idea. I thought it might come in. If it doesn't I'll drop it."

He growled his disapproval. "That's no way—"

It is apparent that he likes a complete outline with all important plot steps made out before you begin to write. But this would cramp me badly. It is the kind of outline I can write only when I have discovered how the characters really want to behave and talk, and this is only evolved when they have been brought to life by being extensively written about. It is in the little things—too inconsequential to have any place in a solid outline—that one sees the beginning of either sorrow or joy.

But the word sorrow, everyone thought, was a bad word to have in a title.

Lippincott was interested in the thumbnail synopsis, and also in a publication date. I had to say I didn't know as to that. I was working hard and feeling better about the book than at any previous time.

"We're jealous of Whit," complained Mark Haverford, "because he gets to see it before we do."

As this was the arrangement they themselves had made, it was a remark that amused me. But boys will be boys.

I wrote Frank: ". . . as to showing some copy, none of it is as yet in final form so what would be the use? Whit hasn't seen any either, only the thumbnail synopsis. When I'm writing well, I don't want anyone to rock the boat . . . I have another title. How would you like *The Devil Enters by a North Window?*"

This interesting title had taken possession of my imagination during a chance conversation with Bertha. (Bertha is Swedish.) She was telling me of a sight-seeing tour she had made in her youth, and how, in that old Scandinavian town, she had seen the big churches of medieval times, built without any window in the north wall, "because the devil enters by a north window."

Surely there was a north window in my book!

One could well imagine that, to the Swedes, all the

evils in existence came from the north—hunger and wolves and howlings of white devastation. . . .

When I talked of this one day to Aroldo, he turned his back to an imaginary north, hunched his big shoulders, sunk his head, and shivered.

Lippincott thought this title "packed a wallop."

But several people said it sounded like the title of a mystery story. This worried me. I envisioned the book jacket designed by an artist with a liking for the spooky— a tall Gothic window, one of the lights ajar, and through this entering a cloven hoof, a bit of a tufted tail, horns. . . . But I thrust the thought away. We would keep the jacket artist well in hand. It was too stunning a title to lose.

Book four had a therapeutic effect on my health. Either I was well again of whatever had ailed me, or merely oblivious of my body.

At any rate, all went well. I worked intensively that winter. The first part of the book became articulated as it never had before. I had about fifteen characters to introduce, whom by this time I knew inside and out. I had already written introductory scenes of the church and the clinic and the Brooklyn house. I was able to put important questions on the board and answer them promptly and easily: Yes, the reader must know about Louise from the very start. Bart does not actually suspect her but is uneasy; he grieves that they have lost some of the closeness and confidence of the early years of their marriage.

The *shape* of my climaxes began to appear. I was able to prepare for them, deliver and retreat from them, writing the proper kind of author-narrative in which to wind them up. My critical sense seemed ready to function when I needed it; I did a lot of cutting. Large pieces of story I had written long ago went right into the book, and it got a bulk at last. And a momentum. When, occasionally, I dumped it on the bed—all those chapters—I was astounded at the mass it made.

I had at last written an introduction of Bartholomew that satisfied me. He was alone. It was the middle of the night. His wife and children were asleep; the unconscious city silent around him except for the constant sounding of the boat whistles. Bartholomew was working at a sermon, his head bent under the reading lamp. His long, nervous hand was upon the manuscript.

I was writing now in a different style.

I do not know how you learn style. I do not really know what it is. You want to say something; your style is the way you say it. It is your way. The way you walk, the way you do your hair, the way you wear your clothes, this is your style. And we all know how very individual it gets to be.

I have read that one's style should be flexible and change according to the material. I agree with that. Would then the style I used in my horse books be the right style for Adam Wyngate? Certainly not. It might have been right for *The Wyngate Children*—semijuvenile —but not for this.

I got a sort of insight about it. Style is not only clarity, wording, phrasing, rhythm, economy, it is also the characterization *of the author.* Yes; the author, omniscient author, is a member of the cast; and must be carefully characterized even though he stands completely outside the story.

For there remains the point of view from which he regards the characters and this imaginary world. He could be in a philosophical mood—and the book would be written in a lofty and contemplative style; or a humorous —and the book would be funny; or he could return to his childhood and the book would be juvenile. His mood, and therefore characterization, can change from chapter to chapter, drenching the very props of the background with his own feeling; and this would change his style more than anything else could change it.

To be able to do this whenever one wants must surely give a writer mastery over a variety of styles. But if one slipped into it unawares . . .

I did this once when I was writing *My Friend Flicka*, and I will tell of it here because it is a perfect illustration of what I mean.

I had sent the first part of the story to Whit and then went for a conference.

I found him very downcast, standing with hands thrust deep in his pockets, head sunk. "It's juvenile. *And I don't know why!*"

As I walked home, I found myself half blind. *Juvenile*. The terrible word enveloped the whole manuscript. It was so vague, any thought of correction was useless. If Whit himself, with the chapters in his hands, had not been able to discover why it was juvenile, how could I hope to?

Well—if I wrote juveniles, then I wrote juveniles. And that was that.

All the same, I had to worry at it. And it wasn't long before I found the funny little trap I had fallen into; also knew that I could quite easily take the juvenility out of it.

I ran to the telephone and passed the good news to Whit. "Don't you see? To write the child scenes convincingly I had to identify myself with the child. Then when the scene ends and I have to do some author-narrative, I haven't yet stopped being the little boy and I go on writing as if I was him and it's juvenile!"

With a bound, Whit seized command. "That's *wrong!* When it's author talking, be as adult as hell!"

Redundant, I thought—wasn't *I* telling *him?*

I can give an opposite instance, when it should have been done and was not, and this was in a book by a very great author, Thomas Mann. The book was *Dr. Faustus.*

He wanted to create the character of a truly exquisite little child, and the story required this. But one sees that the author could not turn into a child himself, not even for a moment. He wrote the scenes completely from a distance—a heavy-footed Jove; and the child, in spite of many such words as beauty, grace, and loveliness, and detailed descriptions of childish postures, continued merely to posture. He never came to life.

Now, here I was faced with the all-important creation of the new and right characterization of Bartholomew, and I needed a new style to write it in.

He had all these children, so they must be there in the book; but he must never get infected with juvenility. I must not get infected myself!

I ran to my library and scanned the rows of books, searching for masculinity. Ah . . . Winston Churchill! And war—the particular business of men. The great soldiers then, and war correspondents—Bradley; Stillwell;

[189]

Pyle. I pulled out an armful of books. I devoured these books. . . .

. . . going better now . . . avoiding the children . . . not bringing them in at all . . . later, when the proper time comes, then I shall get down on all fours and enter the nursery. . . .

Elise came up for a short visit. I gave her my opening pages to read. She is a discriminating reader. I have never known her to like a poor or weak or trashy book.

She read it slowly and put it down and looked at me. "Of course I know nothing about books. I only know how they affect me. If I opened a new book and read those three pages—I couldn't put it down."

Twenty-nine

THE BOOK was now progressing so rapidly I was soon thinking about part two when my Wyngates were all to be at Marshlands for the summer.

A mass of scenes for this part were already written but not as yet in context. Now to get them into context, which means, *writing the story*. And first of all, a short outline. I wrote it and pinned it on the board.

Bart discovers that he does hate his brother. But when he discovers that Ramsey is not Louise's only lover, but that she has had numerous affairs and has never really been true to him, his hate shifts from Ramsey to her. This shows him the truth, namely, that he is not pure. The hatred is in his own heart and simply directs itself toward whosoever has most greatly injured him. Seeing this in himself, he cannot go on in his ministry, healing and teaching others; for obviously, if a man hates everyone who injures him, every enemy, he will always have an enemy to hate.

For a mystic to hate is a contradiction in terms. This breaks him. His mind gives way.

There is the interlude at the mental hospital in Boston where Kristy, the young nurse whom he had once saved from insanity, now is the one to bring him out of this darkness. In the spring he returns to Marshlands and the youngest of his children is sent to him, little Runo, who, of all of them, is most like his father.

All the sketches and outlines of this latter part of the book were easy for me. It seemed work already done, as much of it actually was. It seemed beautiful. I liked it as it went along. It held interest. Bart's emergence from his terrible ordeal, a gradual emergence, and the simple logical steps by which this came about, were convincing. Bart and Louise are eventually united; his family brought together; he can again take up his work.

The reasonableness of this recovery is that he fights the fight out at the true level, which is the innermost. Is it to be hate or love? Is he God's or his own?

And so, here, I reached that point and theme to which I committed myself on U.S. 30 so long ago. I was coming out of the jungle at last—and at the right spot.

I broke it all down into chunks and chapters, found the climaxes, broke the chapters down into plot steps, pausing to write out and pin up many a question. As these were answered, I tore them from the board and threw them away.

The pigeonhole that held *Finished Chapters* would hold no more. I readied another and began to fill that.

Early in April, on a lovely spring day, I had a surprise. Bertha had just brought my breakfast tray. Afterward, the outdoors enticed me. I would steal a bit of this enchanting morning before going back to my desk.

I put on my old garden loafers and began to dig and weed. Presently the telephone rang, and it was Whit and Hallie, saying they were near—on their way up state to see Bill Shirer—and they wanted to stop in and say hello.

This was wonderful news; I wanted a break myself. Joyously, I told them to come right over.

Bertha made one of her superlative soufflés. It was so nice that she likes to be asked, suddenly, for an impromptu luncheon. It creates a pleasant and hospitable atmosphere for everyone.

Hallie is writing another book. . . . I showed them my wonderful desk and Whit took some pictures of me at it. . . . Hallie was tickled when she saw the list of My Faults tacked up on the board. . . . They thought the house had a lot of personality. . . . After lunch we sat on the terrace and talked about *our books.* . . .

Whit had not as yet seen any of this last book four. He wanted to know, with as near a grin as his poker face can accomplish, if anyone else had? I told him no, it was going well, and I was afraid to show it to anyone. He agreed that sometimes it is dangerous.

When I told him about dropping out the romances of the two girls he said, "I always thought you would."

"Yes. I can only write a single-line story. I know that now. But of course lots of writers—and the greatest of them—can handle a number."

"Yes. Tolstoi did. *Anna Karenina* has a dozen stories in it."

He asked me if this book four I was working on now

would be the final book? Or if there would be a book five and perhaps six?

(Ever since I've known him he's been at me about doing a lot of stories at a time. *One at a time, Mary—one at a time . . .*)

I wish I could. But which one? And how am I to know?

We talked about commas, clichés, figures of speech, prepositional phrases.

He asked if I had been doing any reading, and if so what? And when I told him, he exclaimed, with astonishment, "Did you hear that, Hallie? She's been reading about war. The soldiers—"

Thirty

Now THAT I had not only my abstract from start to finish of the book but also the concrete story line, I began to feel as a tired swimmer feels when, after an exhausting swim, his feet just touch the bottom.

The mass of work that remained to be done did not dismay me. It is doubt; it is making bricks without straw; it is the necessity of deciding when you can't decide and have no grounds upon which to decide, that is so demoralizing.

I knew exactly what problems remained to be solved and did not minimize their importance.

1) I still intensely disliked the Ramsey-Joyce relationship, but hoped I would be so clever in my way of dealing with it that I would, after all, enjoy it.

2) I knew that I had to break away from Brooklyn in the middle of the book and go to Marshlands; but had decided I must simply accept this disadvantage philosophically—as many another writer does.

3) I felt my hero had not quite come up to what I had hoped.
4) I felt I had really shirked Ramsey in presenting him in flashbacks.

I pinned these up on the board and stared at them. This very concrete way of facing troubles is always a help to me. Trying to see all around these road blocks, my mind darted hither and thither, and presently I was getting ideas.

Strangely enough, one single alteration in plot—a different opening—solved the last three of these major difficulties with one stroke.

It was an opening that had often occurred to me before, floating across my mind, entering, as it were, from one side, passing across, making an exit at the other side, like a cloud drifting across the sky.

So it had subconsciously been well considered, well tested, and tried. That it kept recurring was significant. When I came to write it, it was like the simple recording of something that had actually happened. And, once written, there was never any need to change it. It was as follows:

Ramsey and his invalid wife, Anna, would come home from Europe on a Saturday morning of midwinter. I had recently had a trip to England and back, so the bringing of a Cunard liner in through the Narrows of the New York harbor was fresh in my mind. I remembered the disappointment of the several thousand passengers when we missed the tide and had to wait over nearly twenty-four hours in the Narrows to catch it on the next morning. I knew the captain and pilot were up there on the bridge, waiting, while the passengers fretted and played bridge (and I thought, envisioning the bringing in of that liner next morning with fog and small fishing boats all around, and a deadline set by the tide, which must turn just as the boat swings into the dock, The men have all the fun).

The docking of the liner would be a scene that would open my book with dignity. It had size and scope. The two great halves of the city of New York deployed there before the reader at the very start. And there was the Brooklyn Bridge, one of the fundamental reasons for my choice of this subject, spanning the river that divided them. Moreover, the slow movement of the big ship as it was warped into the dock, which I felt strongly from the first words onward, set the slow pace. This would hold me down.

The two stallion brothers eyed each other through field glasses, one on the ship, the other on the dock. Bartholomew, with Louise his wife, Edith his older sister, Jennifer his little daughter, had come to meet the returning travelers.

Writing this opening, I seemed to hear a long, deep, sustained organ tone. Now that I had Ramsey right in the foreground of the stage I felt relief. He was indispensable. He would help the interest of the opening a great deal.

Though Bart held Jennifer by the hand, his eyes and his troubled thought were upon his brother; and when he saw his wife blush and avert her face as Ramsey placed a fraternal kiss on her cheek, Bartholomew remembered that there had been something—how much?—between these two in the past.

(Reading this, Aroldo said, "Faint lightnings on the horizon!")

Choosing a Saturday for the opening meant that there would be some sort of social function that evening on Brooklyn Heights. And a church service next morning with Bartholomew preaching; a family dinner at the Wyngate Brooklyn house; some typical Sunday afternoon activity following—all marvelous occasions for the many introductions that must take place.

Earlier than this, in fact immediately following the dock scene, they would all gather for lunch in the private suite Ramsey and Anna had taken at the Waldorf. And here, these three middle-aged people could look at each other, marking the changes that had been made by the years, and remembering their childhood at Marshlands.

And so Marshlands would enter the book, early on; not only with sufficient description by the author, but nostalgically remembered by these three who had been born there and were going to gather there again in the coming summer. After this, Marshlands could never leave the reader's consciousness. Going to Marshlands would seem like going to some familiar place, and there would be no dislocation.

These nostalgic memories would be continued by Edith when she returned home to Brooklyn that afternoon, driving across the Brooklyn Bridge in her carriage with Jennifer by her side.

All this poured out on the typewriter, free writing of the most thrilling kind, one character after the other moving onto the stage in natural and unstudied action.

After the Waldorf luncheon Louise drives off in a hansom cab, having announced that Cecil was having his portrait painted; the governess would bring him over for a sitting that afternoon; she herself must be present to read to him during the sitting. But truth was, she was having an affair with the artist, and she timed her arrival at the studio so that she would see him alone first.

This scene is presented to the reader while Bartholomew goes off to a meeting of the clergy.

Even when I was a small child I was impressed by certain qualities of the Episcopalian clergy. They seemed to me big, jolly, hearty men, most of them good-looking or even handsome. I noticed how they enjoyed their cigars and their jokes and the deep and comfortable armchairs. Such meetings as I described at this point in the book took place fairly frequently in our own household.

The particular presentation of Bartholomew that I longed to deliver, a man nearly always half abstracted in his mystical reflections, emerging suddenly with a vivid and disarming and brilliant smile to meet his neighbor on the mundane level, was here at last on the pages of my book. He was like that. The fact that he was also a most loving and tender father I was going to hold back until much later. I had realized, at long last, how dangerous it was to his characterization to show so soon that at a glance from him a troubled child could turn and rush into his arms. For if you once saw him like that, you could never again think of him any other way; and to most people, he would "come over" as a sort of softy.

In this new opening there was also plenty of opportunity to present the exposition, either in small pieces or a solid chapter. (I questioned which would be best.) For threads of interest led back into the past from almost everything these people said and did.

An opening that delivers the principal introductions, the background, the exposition, and some "faint lightnings" of the story does what I have always felt the beginning of a book should do.

It ran to six chapters; and only then appeared that scene of Bartholomew in his study, meditating his sermon, which had formerly opened the book.

I knew that at last I had got the right opening. It was as when, in doing a puzzle picture, one piece after the other falls into place with a little click.

The deep organ note was struck.

Deep within the story, lying against the very quick of the love-and-hate theme, was the intimate love relationship of Bartholomew and Louise.

During the two years I had been working on the book, I had been writing love scenes for them whenever they occurred to me, and had filed them away to use wherever they would fit in. They were so easy for me I found I had a tendency to forget their importance and allow other material—usually expository (always so difficult to get in) to crowd them off the pages. So I posted a warning on my board:

Watch the trickle-through of the passion theme.

Thirty-one

KENT AND DEIRDRE had begged me to send them the book to read, chapter by chapter, as soon as I had an extra copy. Ann was now typing it for me, with three carbons, beginning at the beginning. It seemed to me it was time I let Kent and Deirdre see it.

It was quite freely discussed by my Monroe friends; it was referred to as The Book. And whether Mary looked well or not, did or did not accept invitations, could open her mouth and talk or had to sit silent with a wild look in her eyes—all was (correctly) referred back to The Book.

But to show it before it was finished was almost as if a mother was not allowed to wait until her infant had ten little fingers and ten little toes, but must expose it prematurely.

How ashamed she would be.

I was ashamed. Though everyone who begged to see it assured me that all would be taken into consideration— they would understand that it was not yet finally revised —they would not judge . . .

And yet they would and I knew it. Though my own

mind may be teeming with corrections and changes that are to come, though the necessity for them is obvious, yet I have seen with surprise that even the most experienced editors sense nothing of this. Well, after all, how could they be expected to?

... they'll land on it ... every little thing. ... But what if they do? You can't *faint* every time anyone looks sideways at The Book. ...

I agreed to send chapters to Kent and Deirdre.

"Do you want me to mark anything I think is wrong, Mother?"

After a long struggle I said, "Put a mark in the margin. A very small mark."

One day Mark Haverford telephoned that he and his wife were driving up the parkway and would stop to see me. I told him I would expect them for lunch.

I knew what this meant. He would want to see some of the book. After three years of writing, how could I refuse?

Besides, I now had this wonderful new opening. Little or nothing would ever have to be done to it or could be. I would defy anyone not to be caught into those opening scenes of Brooklyn and Manhattan, the teeming river, the great liner, and those two brothers, separated for sixteen years, both lovers of the same woman, eying each other through binoculars.

Suddenly I wanted to show it. I examined those thirty pages. There had been typographical errors, some changes and erasures. The critical examination of a manuscript is so important, there should not be anything to distract the eye, to puzzle the reader, or to halt the emotional reaction.

I typed the thirty pages over while I was waiting, and this time there was not an error.

When Mark and his wife arrived, I led them into my room and gave them the copy. They sat down on the chaise longue by the window and I went into the piano room.

I was wondering how close you can come to fainting without actually doing it; reassuring myself, reminding myself that in all my life I never *had* fainted. But as I sat there at the piano, my hands on the keys, playing I did not know what, the room faded out a little.

The first look at them, when they came to rejoin me, told me that the verdict was all I could wish for, because they had that slightly dazed look that one sees on the faces of a theater audience when the curtain has just gone down on a gripping scene.

Mark was flushed. He started walking up and down the floor. "But it's so different from your other books . . . no one would know it was the same author. . . . I wouldn't myself."

He drove his hands deep into his pockets, frowning, studying. "Remarkable! So much more mature . . . remarkable. . . ." He kept saying this over and over, then changed the emphasis. "Re*mar-ar-ar*kable!"

He was still saying this at lunch. Bertha was grinning from ear to ear.

. . . have just glanced back in this journal to see what was the exact date of the Haverfords' visit. It was May 26. It is now July 27. That was two months ago. . . .

What have I done since? Finished section three at a gallop and had to do it over not only once but a dozen times. Re-

[203]

viewed and revised and polished sections one and two so that Ann could copy them.

Kept abreast of her copying, which means proofreading and often making fresh revisions. . . . Work of this kind (critical) holds me up . . . stops my Hot Mind from working. . . .

While I proofread sections one and two, rewrite section three, I am blocking out section four mentally and in notes. . . . Most of the actual scenes of this final section are written; all of the big final scenes between Bart and Louise; but not as yet in context; no story step by step to set them into. . . .

I might as well say here that the book never really recovered from the sudden change of pace it suffered as a result of my reaction to Mark Haverford's inspection of the first thirty pages. I just couldn't settle down. I wrote prodigiously. I felt that nothing much remained to be done. My publisher had read it and liked it.

The bell tolled, warning me: Oh, no? Is there ever a page of really good writing that is "nothing much"? I remembered Harry Hansen's remark, "At the end she wrote as if she was running for a train."

I thought of the publishing company. When Mark got back to the office, he would talk about the book. As a matter of fact Leigh wrote me, "Mark is full of enthusiasm." And the whole force—editors, printers, proofreaders, and then salesmen and booksellers would work together to launch it. It was now a business deal. All the way from Tyrawley to Philadelphia I could feel the gathering of tensions that flung a circle around me and drew me in too. I struggled not to be affected by this. I told myself every day, "Now slow down, slow down."

But I was simply unable to recover the measured pace, the exact rhythm—so long struggled for and with such difficulty achieved—that had been broken when Mark looked at me with fire in his eye and said, "Remar-*ar*-ark-able."

Long letter of criticism from Kent yesterday re the two clergymen walking the Bridge and discussing theology . . . says it drags terribly and follows a chapter that is also draggy. . . . No doubt it is a heavy chapter. . . . What I think is, let those who don't find it interesting skip it. . . . If I didn't put it in, it would seem as if I lacked the knowledge of what two such men would naturally discuss and I don't lack it. . . . Besides, that discussion is fundamental to Bart's actions later in the book. . . . But I'll have to make sure . . . *scan* it. . . .

Kent and Deirdre really doing very well . . . they marked a number of little things I had not caught. . . . They don't like Daisy. I think they're right. I'll change her but it's hard to change a character. I'll change her name, call her Laura—then she'll be different . . . this is important.

Scanned yesterday . . . astounded to find serious drag not Bridge chapter but earlier; opening too long; story held up by Bart's soliloquy on *time* sermon . . . could be shortened and combined with next chapter. . . . Also in chapter seven, over-long retrospect in study . . . made worse by a continued soliloquy in next chapter. . . . Look at your *faults,* Mary . . . too much . . . too much. . . .

Made these changes . . . could hardly bring myself to begin tearing up that first section, now so beautifully typed with carbons . . . sat with my head in my hands a half hour before I could take up scissors. . . . Was testing every step mentally . . . it wouldn't have been the first time I have slashed and cut

[205]

and rearranged only to have to put it all back together again ... fish pieces out of the wastebasket....

Vast improvement ... ought to scan it again but am not yet cold enough on it ... think it is right.... It did not work out as I at first planned ... after several experiments I ended by combining chapters one and two ... inserted between them more about the childhood and the father ... in fact, about half the long expository retrospect that formerly came in chapter seven and seriously halted the story. It belongs earlier, because it is introductory. Also, now, it cuts into fast-moving stuff—Louise's love scene—whereas before it cut into stuff that was already slow. End result is, aside from improving pace and readability, I have nine pages less.... This will help when I get to the Bridge scene ... really getting down to brass tacks now....

Thirty-two

I WOKE on the morning of September 12 and suddenly wished I could do as authors used to do in olden days: *And now, dear reader, if you have borne with me thus far*—and so announce the approaching end.

Once, in a writers' discussion, it was asked, "How do you know when to end a novel?" and I suggested, "When you feel as if you are sliding downhill."

I had often thought writing a novel is like climbing a mountain. You go all the way up, lifting your weight and fighting gravity. You go all the way down again, trying not to slide too fast. Going down is easier.

Henry James said a novel divides itself in half. The first poses the problem; the last solves it. (But since the oak is in the acorn, the first half must contain both the posing and the solving. . . .)

Roughly, my book was to have been in four sections. I was now dealing with the last, but it seemed more like a half than a quarter—the action half; and all that had gone before was preparation. And I certainly felt as if I was sliding.

I wondered if I was just tired of it and wanted to go on to other things? Or still reacting to Mark's enthusiasm?

Kent, Deirdre, and Jonathan were coming for a visit of ten days. I had hoped to have the book finished. Lippincott had hoped also.

... don't trust this sliding feeling ... too much like running for trains. ... Well then fall back on your rule ... say your say; make your point; then quit.

Thomas Wolfe, from all reports, was unable to quit. He could write but he could not stop. I was amazed when I read in the book about Perkins, the editor, and Wolfe, the author, that one fine day Mr. Perkins said, "Now I think we've got enough for a book here, Tom." And they pulled out a long piece of novel like taffy and cut it off.

It seemed to me that Wolfe was not able to deal with plot. He could see and write scenes, marvelous, the very stuff of life forever and forever, until the editor, standing behind him, leaned over and took the pen out of his hand. (Was Perkins Wolfe's Cold Mind?)

But artists are supposed to take the stuff of life and shape it. James wrote "Really, universally, relations stop nowhere, and the exquisite problem of the artist is eternally but to draw by a geometry of his own the circle within which they shall happily appear to do so."

But Wolfe drew no circle. Nor did he take the stuff of life and shape it. He took the stuff of life. Period.

... but it is the most marvelous writing ... perhaps it is even higher art not to shape it but just to get it between the covers of a book like that. ... All the same it approaches the unreadable many times ... as the stuff of life is unreadable! Or so unacceptable—dull, hideous, smelly, endlessly going on and on—! If life was a book one would hurl it across the room. . . .

Well . . . how to end? There's lots more to tell . . . must I deal conscientiously with every plot step or just pinch off the long piece of taffy the way Perkins did and let it go at that? (When he did that in Wolfe's books, there were so many loose ends left hanging that he just jammed them into a long paragraph of flat, wind-up writing and put it in italics and finished the book with that . . . clever.)

No . . . I remember when I used to tell stories to my children . . . they could tell from my voice alone when I was beginning to say *and now, dear reader* (and would shriek in protest). There is that change of tone. Music at the beginning of a piece differs from music in the middle and end . . . and so must a book, if it has shape and rhythm. . . .

Make your point and quit. But it's not so simple as that. At any point in the book I can set down in a few sentences what remains to be said; or, I could spin it out through a thousand pages. . . . Which? Must I take great leaps and arrive at the end? Or continue to spin slowly? And until you know if you are going to say your say in one thousand words or twenty thousand, you can't write one single word. . . .

. . . only one way to answer this . . . get the genuine reaction of a reader to all that has gone before. . . . See if the steady pace must continue, or if there should be the great leaps. . . . *I have to SCAN—* Oh, me! My eyes and brain!

I scanned. I discovered there could be no winding up and no leaping as yet. The steady pace must continue. I felt as though there were a broad and swift-running river within me that had to be dammed and slowed up until it began to flow sluggishly and at last nearly cease flowing.

Only then would I be able to do the proper, lifelike sort of writing.

There were hours, during those days, that I just sat at my desk with my head in my hands, looking inward, leaning with all the weight of my spirit against the push of that river.

Sitting at the typewriter sometimes prevents you from doing your best work. It puts pressure on you. Remove yourself; go out to the garden; or begin to dress; and there is a change in the way the mind works.

How many times I went back and forth, putting the typewriter cover on, taking it off, putting it on, taking it off. . . .

The warning bell tolled.

It tolled all the time. No matter what mental path I ventured upon, thinking, I could do this—or that—or begin here; or deal first with such and such, the bell set up the sort of clangor that warns of imminent catastrophe.

What must be accomplished in this last writing was the gathering up of all the story threads, leading them to their climaxes, delivering the climaxes, and then retreating from them.

The climax of the Bart-and-Louise story, plus and somehow interwoven with the climax of the Ramsey-Joyce relationship. There was also a third (but completely subsidiary) story, namely, that of Jennifer and her older sister Sara. This *could* be resolved, or it could be left hanging. It was not too important.

Moreover, one way or another, Ramsey and Anna had to be got out of the book. I could not do the final scenes between Bart and Louise until those two intruders no longer intruded at Marshlands, or in the family of my protagonist, or even in the reader's mind. Away with them! But how?

Nowhere as yet in the whole book was that scene of violence or death which it needed as an egg needs pepper. I would like the exit of Ramsey and Anna to be accompanied by just the right sort of violence.

One would have thought that my bulletin board, covered with scraps of paper, plot steps, questions, thumbnails, or just things to be remembered, would have given me sufficient direction. Over and over again I studied them all. Here, this one—

Never forget:
The story is Bart's loss of union.

This had drawn me straight through the maze for the best part of the writing. I could really take it down now. Here was another:

Clarification
The principal purpose of revision. The elimination of all that does not contribute to the final effect; and the thorough development and expansion of all that does.

This had helped me trim and cut until now I had arrived at the indispensable. (So I thought.) And here were four questions that had so far not been answered.

1) When does Ramsey claim Joyce as his daughter?
2) Does Louise admit or deny?
3) Does Bart believe or disbelieve?
4) What effect on Joyce?

To answer any one of these seemed to start me off on a new novel.

Beginning to be aware of dreadful brain fag, I stopped studying my board and struggling with story lines. I took the folders with notes for section four into the garden and sat down to read them through. There might be a clue.

It is often a great pleasure to read through my notes, for many of them have been forgotten, and come to me freshly.

I found many a little nugget that made me exclaim in surprise.

In the Perkins book there is the part where, as he read Hemingway's manuscript, he suddenly called people in and cried, "Look! Look here what Ernest has done! This scene, so easy and so simple and so real! Why, anyone could do it!" Then he went on to say that of course anyone could not. It was the most difficult thing in the world to write such scenes and get them in properly.

I found scenes like that in my notes. It made me happy to read them; made me smile. I began to feel a little refreshment and hope again.

Dialogue is written differently nowadays from the way it used to be written. Not long paragraphs or pages of talk, but short, clipped sentences, as if two expert tennis players are playing a swift net game. Such dialogue is not especially true to life, for people are long-winded, repeat themselves endlessly, and seldom are able to say what they mean at the first try, or really shape and finish it at the last. But it is so effective, so much is told with so few words, that the reader is enthralled; his eye sweeps down the page and he has it all at a glance.

Colette is a master of this method.

I found scenes with this sort of dialogue in my notes.

I think what Perkins said, that it is easy and anyone could do it, is true; also true that it is the hardest thing in the world. You don't find too many such scenes in books. They are so convincing they are really just little bits of life cut out. Little vignettes of reality.

To write them, all you have to do is look around and set down what you happen to see, hear, and feel at the moment, and this is easy. What is hard is to provide a context for them, so that you have a right to put them into a book. You must, actually, create a book to hold them.

Such a scene is like a little cockleshell boat tossing on the waves of the river, so light, easy, charming—you cannot look away.

But there has to be the river, which is the book; the stream of story that bears the cockleshell on its breast. And there must be the shore. The permanent, timeless, moveless thing that the river slides past. This gives the story its time divisions—yesterday; today; tomorrow. (Have I stolen this from *Of Time and the River*?)

So here we are back again at the fact that a book must have a beginning and a middle and an end, and each part must feel like itself.

I put away my notes and again looked at those four questions about the Ramsey-Joyce relationship.

I looked at them for a week.

What stopped me flat was that, though I could easily invent plots to answer those questions, every one felt like the beginning of a book instead of the end.

[213]

Thirty-three

... trying to write myself out of this jam. I'm up against the difference between preparatory material and climactic.... The trouble is pace ... the climax or climaxes—for there are several—are emerging, and the pace has quickened, and yet there is too much to tell at that speed....

Ah! Look there! I said climaxes ... *plural.* ... Now I'm getting to the heart of it. ... How can one deal with a number of climaxes coming one right after the other without writing the kind of stuff that would make Ripley say, *Really awfully bad?* ...

... how did I get all these climaxes? Well, they are in my notes for section four.... I have been saying to myself all along, When I get to section four it will be plain sailing because I've got so much good stuff. ...

Once my attention was focused on the technical problem, that of building to and delivering a single effective climax, I began to feel relief. A climax is hard for anybody.

I had studied it in my screen work, and I had studied it with Donald Jordan in my lessons in composition. I

[214]

could remember his pointing out when he was once examining a composition of mine that the music was just "going on and on" whereas, having begun to climb for a climax way back *there,* it must continue climbing until the climax has been reached. All else must be dropped out.

Climaxes, he said, were the most difficult part of any composition. They were like icebergs, the greater part—the preparation—behind and underneath and invisible. (Donald should know, since his symphonic works have been played by the best orchestra in the country.) I found it fascinating to pick out, under his direction, those notes, chords, short passages that began, long in advance, to give notice of the climax that would eventually appear.

It would be the same with my book. But first I had to know where I was going. The scene of violence would, it could be presumed, be near the end. Bypassing, for the time being, the whole climax of the Ramsey-Joyce affair, if I could determine the scene of violence, I might work back from that.

I had a whole folder of scenes of violence written. I examined them. Death by drowning; a sail in a boat that has been set on fire; Anna dying under the knife in a hospital; or, possibly, one of the children dying. I thought of Cecil, for Louise idolized this oldest boy. His death would alter her whole nature.

That no one would die during the time span of such a group history seemed unlikely. There was certain to be violence somewhere. And why would it not come to one of these careless, reckless children, most likely to Cecil, who did not know what fear was?

In case any reader of these pages is as pained as my son

when omnipotent author talks of killing off this one or that one, and points out that critics refer to me as ruthless, I answer that I must write of death as I see it; to be taken with a grain of salt; not so important; not the end. A door out—and a door in.

When a character makes an exit, it is only a stage that is abandoned. I am in good company when I say that life is a play or a dream. And once you know that, you can lay the burden of it down and walk lightly.

So I encouraged myself to think of fatal accidents. Then I realized it was impossible. For if one of those children died, no reader would care any more about anything that happened to Bart and Louise. I was astounded that I could have considered it. But such decisions are not obvious until they have been made.

Then it might be Anna who died. Unless it were the devil himself, Ramsey; or both of them. An automobile accident.

I found in my notes the description of a shocking accident that had happened in California. A car had gone over a cliff, killing all the occupants except one. This one was reached by a rescue crew, but as he was being drawn up to safety, one of those carrying the stretcher had slipped. The injured man was dropped and this time killed.

Then as the engineer of the insurance company stood on the cliff edge, directing the job of salvaging the car, one of the cables snapped, looping upward to snare the engineer, snatch him off into the air, and hurl him down onto the rocks.

I found this a very intriguing episode. Ramsey would

be driving the car full of ladies. They would stop at the cliff edge to admire the view. It would be when he cranked it, having forgotten that he had left it in gear, that it would charge him and hurl him over the cliff.

I wrote several versions of this to see how it would feel. It did not feel very good.

However, I had now linked Ramsey and automobiles in my mind. They seemed to fit together. And there resulted from this thinking a good deal of "business" for Ramsey that had to do with an automobile. I went way back in the story and fitted this all in, even an episode when an automobile that was in gear was to be cranked. The victim would have been Bart, not Ramsey.

But none of this gave me a good finish for Ramsey. I really did not know what to do with him.

The getting of truth and reality into a piece of fiction is a strange business. Just putting in factual happenings does not serve at all. The action about the car going over the cliff, was all facts, but it had no reality. I knew in my heart that Ramsey did not go over the cliff.

But there are many different sorts of actual happenings, and before I finish with a book I demand of myself that I shall have discovered the *true* thing that *did* happen; even that my whole story must have happened at some place, some time, and even many times.

Kent once wrote me from Wright Field that a young officer said to him, "I heard you are the son of the author of *My Friend Flicka*. I wanted to meet you because, you know, that happened to me. I had a little horse that got injured and lay in the stream. And I found it and spent the night there in the water, just the way the little boy in the book did."

This was very exciting for me to hear. I wrote Kent, "Ask him if it was a filly? Ask him if it got well?" And the answer to both questions was, Yes.

That same question of the truth or falsity of something I had put in *My Friend Flicka* came up in Whit Burnett's classroom when they were discussing the story. No one thought the filly could have recovered.

The story had been read anonymously. Whit suddenly got impatient and roared, "Tell us, Miss O'Hara. Did the filly really get well? Or didn't she?"

Every head whipped around to look at me, and I had to answer, "No, she died." There was an uproar. They had all been sure of it, and I could hardly make myself heard as I insisted, "But I always believed she would have got well if only I had known and could have got down there to the stream to hold on to her."

Silence fell upon the roomful of students. After a moment or two Whit conceded it. "And that's your story."

And then they all conceded it.

What I had to do now, was to know that Ramsey was a real person; he had lived; a thousand Ramseys had lived; he was as I had described him. Now—what happened to him?

It took me a good many days to discover that nothing of a disastrous nature happened to Ramsey. Ramsey was one of those who are punished by getting just what they want.

And what did he want? To be master. To dominate. To carry everything before him. To outdo and make nothing of Bart. To possess everything of value. To be looked up to and envied.

A bit of neat plotting was necessary here, going way back into the book; something that would ring true with everything that had been written about the two brothers, their parents, their early life. The moment I hit upon it I knew it was right.

Ramsey must be illegitimate himself; not the son of Adam Wyngate, but of that Darcy cousin with whom his mother, Charlotte Ramsey, had lived, as an adopted sister, before she was married. The wealthy Darcys had had that fabulous southern estate, Ligonier, and there Ramsey had actually had his beginnings.

. . . yes, history repeats itself . . . first Charlotte married to Adam, gives birth to a son (Ramsey) who is not Adam's . . . and then Louise gives birth to a daughter (Joyce) who is not Bartholomew's. . . .

Who was it who said that life has a horrible symmetry? It sounds like Henry James. This plot had that horrible symmetry. The longer I thought about it the more certain it seemed.

And the end of Ramsey would be when, by some means, he becomes master at Ligonier. The means would be Anna. If he had access to Anna's millions, he could buy Ligonier when it comes on the market and lord it there forever. But Anna guarded her millions. Then it was Anna who must die. So exeunt Ramsey and Anna.

This would mean, of course, an enormous rewrite from the very beginning of the book. For wherever Ramsey came in, or people talked about him, there must be just a touch or a word or a glance, to keep the reader aware of who Ramsey really was. I had no intention of delivering this as a surprise, which would simply burden the end of my book with one more climax; this was to be part of Ramsey and his place in the book from the very beginning. It was a premise of the story. The reader must know it as easily, as undramatically, and as early on as possible. And I felt that the mere fact that this could be done without disturbance of any other characters or situations proved that it really was the truth. He was Bart's half brother. Bart was the real master of Marshlands.

Before daring to tackle such a big rewrite I ran down to New York and spent several days with Reese. At cocktails, at dinner, and after dinner, we discussed episodes of this kind that we had both known or heard of. A lawyer is invited to inspect many strange domestic tangles.

When I drove home again, I was thinking of my horribly symmetrical irregularity as quite a mild one after all. And I was jubilant at the amount of clutter I had now removed from my final section.

Ramsey's return to Ligonier would cut short any great involvement over Joyce. He would hardly care if she was his daughter or not. He would go through with that scene I had written so long ago, in which he put the terrible suspicion in Bart's heart, but it would be primarily to crush his brother and triumph over him one last time.

Thirty-four

So BACK to the beginning again with scissors and pins and glue; juggling, rewriting, scanning, and ever more scanning, for it's one of the most difficult things to do without the patches showing, once the story has been written in continuity and all the parts articulated.

But there was peace to it, not worry. It was drudgery only.

The worry was there on my board. Still those same questions, still unanswered.

1) When does Ramsey claim Joyce as his daughter?
2) Does Louise admit or deny?
3) Does Bart believe or disbelieve?
4) What effect on Joyce?

These represented the irreducible minimum of what my story yet had to unfold.

I thought in desperation of dropping out the whole business. I had often thought of this before. Here I was on page four hundred and fifty. If I went on with this complication it would take several hundred pages more. The book would never hold it. Did I have any choice?

But the pivot of the whole story was Bart's hatred turning from Ramsey to Louise. How else could I make that convincing? Besides, why else was Joyce even in the book now that she had lost her love, her organist?

The warning bell tolled. It shook me with its mighty tollings.

I felt as if I was engaged in a death struggle with the book. My thoughts swept back to the opening scenes, the first mention of Joyce in the first chapter, and shudders shook me. Suppose there was something untrue there, in the very beginnings and underpinnings of the story?

One of the inherent difficulties of writing is that you must plan in advance what your goal is; then approach it. But when you get close, you see that if you follow the rule *What would they naturally do?* you would not arrive at that goal at all. Well then, must you throw away all your work and begin again? Donald used to say, "In a way, you have to write it all at once." (Stravinsky, he told me, begins in the middle and works both ways.)

Of course. How can you take the first step on the path till you know where you are going? How can you know where you are going until you or at least your mind starts going there?

I went on with the other work, the shudders still shaking me, the bell still tolling. If Joyce was not true . . .

Lippincott wanted—they very much wanted a publication date. I wrote them that I was on the final rewrite.

Leigh came to call on me, very eager. We talked jackets, promotion, blurbs, and at last he came out with the principal purpose of his visit.

They didn't want Whit to see any of it before they did.

Had he seen it? No! Would I not be willing to give them a copy at least as soon as Whit received his? "After all, we're the ones who are going to publish it. . . ."

I had to laugh. I roared. He got laughing too. I told him the truth, that no one had seen any of this book four except Mark and that he had seen only the first thirty pages; that Whit had seen nothing since I had shown him the first hundred pages of *The Wyngate Children* and that was a year and a half ago and was not this same book at all. I had had no conferences with him since then, because there was no fundamental uncertainty in my mind as to how to write it.

My plan was, I assured him, to send off two copies simultaneously, one to Lippincott, one to my special editor.

But I demurred at setting a deadline. I was writing as fast as I could. It was going well. It was nearly finished.

Now Kent and Deirdre and Jonathan came on for their visit.

Jonathan is as beautiful as the Wyngates and very bright. He tried to say Jonathan and achieved Jody, which he has remained. He tried to say Hara and achieved Hydie, which I have remained.

There was a rule that until noon no one was to enter my room. But he would present himself at the door, and in a voice as high and sweet as a white-throat sparrow, chant, "Whay-ah Hydie?" Then, triumphantly, *"They*-ah Hydie!" And then, "Hydie! Hydie! Hydie! Hydie!"

Marvelous crescendo to a climax.

I bought a small chair, a Lilliputian chair, and hid it

under another chair. Almost hid it. Give him something to discover and tug at.

And yet with all of this going on, I worked steadily, and the long rewrite about Ramsey was finished by October 1, when Kent and Deirdre returned to Dayton.

I had made a contract with myself. If those four questions had not answered themselves by the time all my other work was done, I would force myself. And now the other work was done, and the questions were still unanswered.

I set the time.

. . . it shall be this morning . . . within the next half hour. . . . I'll make the typewriter answer them . . . set them down and write something instantly, if it's only a nonsense sentence or a row of dashes. . . .

1) When does Ramsey claim Joyce as his daughter? *Ans.* Just before he leaves Marshlands. (*That's odd—a sort of parting shot. . . .*)

2) Does Louise admit or deny? *Ans.* She denies, of course. (*But what of it? She denies everything always.*)

3) Does Bart believe or disbelieve? *Ans.* Either or neither. (*It's just a drop in the bucket to poor Bart; no way of proving or disproving anything.*)

4) What effect on Joyce? *Ans.* I haven't the least idea. (*That would be another book.*)

It was a serious shock to me when I sat looking at what I had written and realized what it meant. The Joyce-Ramsey business was out.

I stood up and put the cover on my typewriter. I got into a hot bath as quickly as I could because I was having chills and shivers.

Whatever was I going to do with Joyce? Every scene in the whole book in which she appeared was based on the fact of her relationship with Ramsey and aimed at this final denouement.

The whole book began to totter.

An hour later I was in my car with Kim, driving up Route Seven, once more headed for Tyringham and Elma's place there among the pines.

She had been asking me all summer to come up for a visit. Wheels under me would help me to think.

But I couldn't think at all. Every effort I made to scan mentally, to move parts of the story around and see what changes I could make, failed. My mind just fell away. At last I gave up.

I saw that if Joyce was not the particular girl, with the particular trouble and destiny that I had given her, then she would be a different girl with a different problem and destiny. The job I was shirking was changing her into that totally different person, changing her appearance, all she said and did and was; beginning again, actually, to create a new character and, for *some* reason, insert it into my nearly finished book and integrate it. . . . For *what* reason?

It was not until I was driving home, two days later, that I realized I need not change her, just eliminate her. Almost in the same split second that I thought of it, I did a mental scan from the first page to the last, saw that it could be done, and that it was true.

Home again . . . much quieter in mind . . . this is right. Should I work out the end now? It won't be hard with all the complications out of the way.... Or begin the enormous rewrite ... doing completely over every chapter in which Joyce appears or is spoken of? ...

What I did do was, quite suddenly, to write that whole chapter in which Ramsey lies on the bed letting his wife die. Here, at last, was my scene of violence. A murder story after all. And a very original murder.

This death scene went so easily, seemed so right, cleared up so much, it gave me support for all the rest. It seemed like a great strong beam reinforcing all the final structure.

So exit Anna.

Thirty-five

I worked long hours. But again it was just work, not worry. I was at peace. I was exultant. But, oh, how weary.

I had the concrete plot of the last section clear to the end now, every plot step typed in a single sentence and pinned on the board. It remained to decide how much length to give them.

Excising Joyce proved not to be difficult. Strange how tenuously she moved through her scenes. Once again the girl of excessive beauty had met tragedy. She lost first her love, then her very self.

But as I went through those early chapters of the book I was alarmed to find how many errors there still were. There were discrepancies in the character of Edith, who, at the end of the book, played an increasingly important part. This meant her early scenes had to be altered and strengthened in preparation for this.

Some chapter breaks were wrong. Here and there organization not of the best. And still it dragged.

I had been saying to myself all along that, of course, it would need cutting. But now, emerging from my author-cocoon and taking into my mind other people's thoughts, I scan with much more objectivity and slash more ruthlessly. I can just hear Whit say, always with his poker face, "They won't read it—they won't read it."

I broke one great mass into two chapters and reorganized. I took out two long reflections of Bart. I made all the first part far more readable, and at the same time never ceased work on the finish.

Climactic writing is always difficult; exact timing so important. Just where the breaks? How long can those leaps be that take the plot from one peak to the next?

Most of the scenes were written and were good. Those that still had to be written went on wings. Free writing was mine to command whenever I needed it. For the pure love of it I did scenes several times over; try them this way; then try them that. . . .

I myself have never liked a book to end too abruptly the moment the point has been made. When I hear that tone of voice— "And now, dear reader—" I want to protest, as my children did. It is inhuman. You cannot be cut off so quickly from people you have come to love and that magic world they live in. You want to accompany them in that quiet period of their lives when things go well instead of ill, when nothing threatens.

I planned a longer finish. I gave myself fifty pages, then remembered that Jane Austen allows herself only a page and a half in which to say *So they lived happily ever after.* So I did it more briefly; too briefly; and I had to rewrite all, at a still slower pace, before the book actually came out.

... still trying to cut ... this is an awfully long book. ... Wondering if I'll have room to get in that twenty-page block that makes a separate drama of the struggle between Sara and Jennifer ... I've some good scenes written for that. ...

... don't know about the length after all ... anything under five hundred pages seems to me would be all right. ... It's a big story about big people and a lot of them. ... Look at *The Caine Mutiny*, 494 pages; *The Cardinal*, 579; *The Cruel Sea*, 510; *The Wall*, 632.

To know when a book is finished is as difficult as knowing when a calf becomes a cow. In answer to telephone calls from Lippincott I answer, "Why, yes, it's finished—*practically* finished. ..."

Mark came by for lunch one day and was disappointed when I said I couldn't give him the manuscript. I begged for a few more days.

... still finding discrepancies ... here and there an omission ... so much revision makes this likely. ... Also found Joyce's name again and again ... nothing but a name now, poor child, but still that trace of her lurking as if you'd find a freshly perfumed handkerchief lying by a chair in a room that had not been occupied. ...

My warning bell told me the book needed several more stone-cold scannings. I've often thought I'd like to turn in a book so thoroughly scanned for once, so completely polished and finished that no one would even want to change a comma. But you have to wait and cool off between scannings; and what author can wait so long right at the end? What publisher would let her?

. . . I'm toning it down a little here and there . . . taking out some of the drive . . . how much to leave in? I remember that Brahms cooled off for about ten years before he made the final revisions of his symphonies, and then what he did was take out the extremes. (Take out the exclamation point and put a period. Take out those adjectives and adverbs, very, extremely, the best, the worst, take out underlinings and let the word stand without accent or emphasis.) Brahms changed three FFF to FF. And two FF to F. Not so much *issimo*. . . .

. . . well, it's going off soon. . . . Ann and I working incessantly copying pages that look messy. . . . Every time I copy a page I change a word or two . . . don't like that. . . .

When I was writing *My Friend Flicka*, I made a rule that I would read each finished page aloud, looking for errors; and if I changed so much as one word, would do it again; would keep doing it until I had read it aloud three times without wanting to change even a comma.

I did not forget this now, but I just didn't have the courage. It would hold up the delivery of the book for at least a couple of months.

Besides, I knew I could keep working on it even after I had delivered it. And the editors would have their blue and red pencils out too. On such a monumental book there were bound to be a great many blue and red marks.

Telephone calls kept coming in from friends and family. Have you finished it yet? Sent it?

Long distance from Kent and Deirdre at Dayton.

I wondered if I could get the manuscript into the box the typewriting paper came in. Ann and I experimented with this.

I would send Whit's copy by mail; carry the Lippincott

copy to their New York office in person. Spend that night at Reese's apartment.

"And we'll celebrate with champagne," telephoned Reese. "We'll toast the book!"

"And the *Tinavire!*" I said.

Kent planned to fly on for the occasion if the champagne could be at midnight. In my mind's eye I saw us around Reese's table holding up our champagne glasses, Kent in his blue Air Force uniform. . . .

Whit's copy went into the mail on October 16, 1951, the day before I went down to New York.

I went to the Lippincott office with the big box under my arm. There was good-natured rivalry amongst the three editors, but it was agreed that Mark should read it first, then Frank, then Leigh.

This being Thursday, I figured that Mark would read it over the weekend and I *might* hear from him Monday. Or Tuesday.

Then Frank would take a full week. I might hear from him the following Monday, October 28.

As for Whit—

. . . why, Whit has it already . . . may be sitting reading it this moment . . . blue pencil in his hand of course. . . . I could hear from him any moment. . . . If I've succeeded in doing what I wanted to do with this book, it isn't a book you put down once you start it. . . . Whit will read it at a sitting. . . .

Thirty-six

I CAME BACK from New York the next day minus the big package under my arm and the big world in my head. I had that feeling you have in flying dreams—so light you're going to take off any moment.

I stopped at my roadside mailbox, thinking there might be a note in it already from Whit, but there was nothing, not even the telegraphed acknowledgment of the receipt of the manuscript. I was certainly expecting that.

I began to worry a little as to whether or not it had safely reached him in his little hideaway editorial offices at Setauket, Long Island. This was Friday, October 18. Just a week later I wrote:

. . . still on the anxious seat . . . not a word, *not one word* from anyone. . . . Very hard to go about emptying wilted flowers out of vases, putting fresh ones in, ordering meals, attending to mail, all as if something important, *the world* were not impending. . . .

Have fallen into a complete tailspin . . . it's no good. . . .

Scanned mentally . . . chin up again . . . it's good . . . have

[232]

just sent Whit wire as follows: Did you receive manuscript registered mail one week ago? have had no word. . . .
. . . don't feel very well . . . I've got pains. . . .

At ten o'clock I received Whit's answering wire: "Acknowledged receipt of manuscript week ago. Already working on terribly interesting book. If can drop all other work hope to see you Monday, November 5."

There was some relief when I received this. At least the manuscript had not been lost—only the wire of acknowledgment. But to any author, I imagine the news that an editor is "working on" his book, is something of a blow. Careful reading of course, marginal notes, suggestions or opinions set down on another sheet to be talked over—all that would be expected and would somehow carry a totally different impression than "I'm working on your book"; especially when it is coupled with the fact that this work is going to consume more than two weeks, specifically, from October 18 to November 5, even though all other editorial work is dropped.

And, from that wire, I could not even tell if he liked the book or not. That it was "terribly interesting" said nothing. I wondered if he had read it. He always has a lot of work on hand. He might not have been able to get at it yet.

I was in utter misery that morning.

I thought of Thomas Wolfe. Poor Thomas Wolfe, who, when his book was finished, simply could not face it, and turned and ran for Europe. He was in London when the magnificent reviews began to appear.

If I had only known it, I was then within an hour or two of deliverance.

Our mail is put into the big tin box with *TYRAWLEY* painted on it at about one o'clock every day. I was out there (it may be taken for granted) soon after the mail automobile pulled up at the box.

I stood there on that lovely October day, shuffling through the letters, and saw no telegram, no letter with either the Story or Lippincott letterhead. There was, however, one letter with a hand-addressed envelope. The writing seemed familiar.

I tore it open and saw that it was signed Mark. He had written his letter by hand, instead of dictating it to a secretary, had written it at his country house outside of Philadelphia.

I read the letter through without moving away from the mailbox. As soon as I finished it I read it through again; and again; and again. At last I could fold it, put it back in its envelope, lift my head, and look around. I realized that my load was lifted. The whole burden of that book and all the long writing of it had fallen from me, and was never to oppress me again.

It was a letter of the highest praise, commendation, and congratulation. It was, in fact, an elaboration of what he had said in my own house, walking up and down my living room, particularly expressing his surprise at the ability I had shown to change my style from near-juvenile writing to this picture of mature characters.

Presently I was hurrying back to my typewriter to write him "... good words, dear Mark. ... Bertha and I were in the doldrums. ... She clutched her heart every time the telephone rang. ..."

A few hours later came the following telegram from

Whit: "This is your biggest and finest book so far stop terribly excited about it and hope to see you in a few days. Whit."

And the telegram was almost immediately followed by this letter:

DEAR MARY,

I don't think it will be necessary for me to tell you how good a book you have written. No one could have written a book like this without, at the end, realizing the stature of it. It is a very fine and a very big novel, in the best tradition of a created world peopled with human beings, seen from many points of view by a creator who has been able to see all around them and through them, and to assemble them at a point in time and place in the best possible manner to set them off against their background.

I thought you wrote about horses, and people had been brought in almost needlessly, because you did the other job so well. I see now that the domestic and human relations of people have been in the back of your mind for a long, long time. All that observation and reflection has now poured forth in a very rich book indeed, and probably at no time in your own life and experience could you have given as deep going, as satisfying, as strong and as sympathetic a picture of people as you have done in this book and at this time. It plays on many levels, and each level seems to me important and revealing, and the craftsmanship in this book is so good one relaxes as before a first rate orchestral director, knowing that his reading of the score will be right because the confidence is there in the conductor.

I have made a small penned dot along the right or left hand margin of the pages from about page 2 to 613, so I will not bother giving the line reference on the page, and probably each query I have made will be clear to you when you see the dot.

There are a few generalities that might be mentioned here, before specific lines come up. I am sure some people may think the book is too long. Where that feeling may come from perhaps, is in a possibility that some of the theological discussions get a little abstract for a general reader, although I myself feel that this theorizing is invaluable as a contrast to the human actions later. I have questioned several places whether it is not actually anachronistic in 1904 to have so many specific references to Eddington, Freud, and the cyclotron, the latter not even being in my complete Webster dictionary as late as the 1934 edition. I felt there was too much space given to Mary Baker Eddy's theories, and I have suggested trimming here, since I thought this particular sect got out of focus, and will be offensive to many, anyway.

The craftsmanship with which you withhold the interior of the mind and nature of Louise and Ramsey, revealing Ramsey's conception of himself no earlier than at the death of Anna, which is almost the end of the book; and not revealing the real sexual nature of Louise until even later—provides a psychological suspense in the book that is almost like the unraveling of a mystery. You have kept her enigmatic, presented her as a normal mother and as a liar and deceiver, and not completely overbalanced the scales in one direction or the other.

I think the combination of spiritual and sexual struggles that we have through this book is a very powerful one, and that you have gradually pulled off the layers of convention from an absorbing group of people, and that the success you have had in allowing us to see this book peopled with adults and their problems as well as children and their problems,

[236]

without the adultness coming too close to the children, is a triumph of skill.

You have shown a strength in facing scenes such as I had not believed you had, in spite of my admiration for your capacities. The scene of Anna, attempting to crawl back to her room from the country inn bathtub down the hall, and the whole treatment of her illness that night, is as ruthless as anything I have ever read, and I think as true.

The fishhook in the eye of Runo is almost too painful to read, and of course the Easter singing of Cherry and Cecil is heartbreaking. You have "played it big."

There are dozens of scenes that I have the greatest admiration for, which I can tell you about when I see you personally, but this would be merely praise, and not of very much help. The thing is, you have done a book in period, with all its sights and sounds and smells; you have given us a Brooklyn and a Maine summer place, filled with people of good manners and bad habits; a book of growing children and fumbling adults, and all of them meaning well and trying to adjust themselves to their natures, their strivings and the splits in the personalities.

These skeletons, however properly clothed, have been viewed with an artist's detachment, and upon analysis it is remarkable how disarmingly you have worked them out of their closets. This book, in the amours, deceptions, hypocrisies and other evils of human nature, is as modern and ruthless as anything of the youngest generation of contemporary writers. The difference here is, the evils are not paraded, but are concealed. The society here is a kind of tapestry, behind which these characters at times attempt to hide, and not a garment they are constantly attempting to throw off.

I felt that while you were withholding the real nature of Louise, she was for me at least for quite a long time a completely faceless woman, and not until very late on do you actually give a visual impression of her face, and that as doll-like, which it seems to me ought really to occur almost in the first discussion of her, or at least at some point where Bart is studying her face as such.

The Jack Drummond chapter seems necessary although wherever you think some trimming could take place, I am sure it would not be amiss.

I think the purgatorial sections are very strong.

This is a very long book, but my own feeling is to let it stand. There may be too many stories within stories, but each contributes something, and since this is a book Victorian in its mood and late Victorian in its actual happening in time, I would advocate letting it run full, except for cuts I have suggested, and let the reader skip if he feels like it. I am a hard cutter, but there is so much revealing material of a sound nature in this book that I am a little baffled as to what really could come out, if word count is the most important thing.

I was put off and recaptured again and again by dramatic devices which I admire your so effectively using. The rough sea is a threat, and the two men swim but they come in un-harmed, but the next time they swim it is something else again. Cecil races the train but reins up at the crossing unhurt, but a few days later is hurt on a horse.

You can see from all this that it would be a pleasure to rattle on for a long time about this book. It is a very impressive job. You have pulled it off. It is your best book to date. It is perceptive and powerful. You have met every scene, and the net result is a book on the grand scale, and a very interesting moment in American morality, and the flirt who marries the minister is an unforgettable portrait, but her husband is a vastly bigger one. It is not merely a woman's book, but a book of a family and period and a society, and a strange wrestling with the devil in the flesh from which neither the woman nor this spiritual son of Adam can free themselves.

Congratulations!

Sincerely,

Whit

I have been told by a discriminating reader that for me to set down the above letter without accompanying it with those already mentioned disclaimers to the effect that of course I did not "lap up" all the praise would lay me open to accusations of conceitedness.

Alas—I fear I did lap it up. And every review that gave me more praise. And grieved at those that did not.

Who would not do the same?

Thirty-seven

And now, dear reader . . .

The few remaining adventures of this particular novel can be told briefly.

J. B. Lippincott Co. rejected it.

Whit and Hallie Burnett, who had left Dutton's some time since, were now associates and editors with the David McKay Company. At Whit's suggestion I submitted the manuscript to McKay, and received the following telegram: ". . . very much impressed with the Wyngate novel and feel this is a major work of real importance stop will wire you Friday with what we believe will be an interesting offer for the publication of the book. Kennett L. Rawson." I accepted their offer.

Once again, a novel of mine was to carry the Story Press imprint.

Why Lippincott rejected the book has remained a mystery. Obviously they did not like it enough or have sufficient confidence in it to publish it; this has not quieted speculation. I am still asked the question, and still have to reply that I haven't the least idea. All I knew was that one member of the board was enthusiastic about it, but one does not make a majority.

Actually, the novel was not yet in completely finished form.

I have written that the ending of the book never recovered from the abrupt change of pace that took command after Mark read the opening. I did it over many times, expanding, adding facts, feelings, explanations, slowing it down. But almost before the script had left my hands, I realized I had not slowed it down enough. I was not surprised when, at the first conference with the McKay editors, they complained of the galloping finish. Fortunately I had a new revision ready. Now, two years later, I wish I could do it yet again.

I have read that Chopin never permitted himself to be swerved from his determination to hold off publication until he was *sure* on every smallest point; and to arrive at that sureness sometimes took him ten years. This, it was said, accounted for the fact that, to a degree attained by few others, his works stand perfect and unalterable.

I remember that when President Wilson announced his Fourteen Points to the world, offering them as a basis for international agreement, an answer came (from India, of course) asking if he had given sufficient time to the weighing of these Fourteen Points? And "sufficient," the polite suggestion was, could hardly be less than a year for each Point?

But time is short in America. Publication for Adam Wyngate was set for March 30, about five months after acceptance.

The McKay editors (we were a group of five) worked

[241]

continuously for those three months. All those questions I had left open— Must the book be drastically shortened? Should all the sermons stay in? Should any of the case histories be taken out? —were settled.

The manuscript was "trimmed." This is an interesting process, the taking out not only of every large chunk that can be spared, but half paragraphs, half sentences, as well as single words. Of course I had been doing this all along, but an author's feeling is not so coldly impersonal as an editor's. Showers of my words went into the wastebasket. I felt no regret. It was all to the good, except in the case of certain deletions that I felt altered the style, and here I stood to my guns.

There were also corrections.

The character of Edith had become more important as the book neared its end. I needed someone to do and say important things, Edith was there, I used her to do them. But I had not foreseen this from the beginning, or planned it. And so I found I had to go backward in my manuscript and, in every scene where Edith appeared, give her different things to say and do. What I had already done of this did make Edith come over to the reader as a strong and likable character, but I had not done enough. The editors caught inconsistencies, and I rewrote it, and was glad to, for this was a serious flaw.

I had left another question open for final talks with the publisher; that of the opening.

Early in this book I discussed the two ways of getting in the exposition—the old way and the new way.

The old way, speaking broadly, was to begin the novel with action taking place in the *present*. Then, later, probably in Chapter Two, go backward in time and give the necessary *past* history of the characters.

Forcibly to dislocate the reader from the present to the past, and then from the past back to the present again, gives him a shock. Every author hates to do it. Yet it must be done. Should it be done once for all and then no more (the old way)? Or should it be done over and over again, bit by bit throughout the book (the new way)?

I have used both these methods and have never been able to decide which is best. One finds examples of both ways in the best modern books.

In the case of Adam Wyngate, I decided to do it the old way, quite prepared to have this challenged. It was. Mc-Kay editors preferred the new way.

This meant a great deal of rewriting for me, as it is something that must be most carefully done—the chopping apart of present action to insert past action—but there was nothing here I had not well considered in advance, and I had no fear that it would hurt the book.

Wishing to get the feeling of readers on the subject of these two methods of opening a book, I asked a number. Almost all preferred the new way, the reason being that, if it is only a short insertion, they can skim through it, catch the sense, and be back again in the stream of *present* action without actually having allowed themselves to be wholly drawn into the *past*.

So many said this that I think I shall have to yield the point.

And so the work went on until the very day of printing.

The book went almost immediately on the best-seller lists, where it remained for twenty-two weeks.

Two more favorable comments must be quoted, and the reader will know why. Fanny Butcher, in the *Chicago Tribune,* wrote of Bartholomew ". . . incidentally, one of the few really convincing mystics in modern literature."

And the famous European editor, Dr. Max Tau, wrote from Oslo, Norway, "Your books are among the best American literature can give to the old world, as you have a connection with the origin of nature and of the human being, and a warmth which can give us strength."

There are certain tributes that create no pride at all, but humility and gratitude, and permit one to write *finis* with a deep and very wonderful peace.

116 BS Ap. 15 '52 p. 14

"Son of Adam Wingate will not be hailed
as a major contribution to American
letters, but it will be popular
with a certain not inconsiderable
audience, for whom it will do more
good than harm."